Internal Accounting Systems and Controls

Workbook

Sheriden Amos

Published by Osborne Books Limited
Tel 01905 748071
Email books@osbornebooks.co.uk
Website www.osbornebooks.co.uk

Design by Laura Ingham

Printed by CPI Group (UK) Limited, Croydon, CRO 4YY, on environmentally friendly, acid-free paper from managed forests.

British Library Cataloguing in Publication Data
A catalogue record for this book is available from the British Library

ISBN 978-1-911198-73-4

Contents

Introduction

Chapter activities

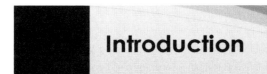

Introduction

Qualifications covered

This book has been written specifically to cover the Unit 'Internal Accounting Systems and Controls' which is mandatory for the following qualifications:

AAT Level 4 Diploma in Professional Accounting

AAT Diploma in Professional Accounting – SCQF Level 8

This book contains Chapter Activities which provide extra practice material in addition to the activities included in the Osborne Books Tutorial text, and Practice Assessments to prepare the student for the computer based assessments. The latter are based directly on the structure, style and content of the sample assessment material provided by the AAT at www.aat.org.uk.

Suggested answers to the Chapter Activities and Practice Assessments are set out in this book.

Osborne Study and Revision Materials

Additional materials, tailored to the needs of students studying this unit and revising for the assessment, include:

- **Tutorials:** paperback books with practice activities
- **Student Zone:** access to Osborne Books online resources
- **Osborne Books App:** Osborne Books ebooks for mobiles and tablets

Visit www.osbornebooks.co.uk for details of study and revision resources and access to online material.

Acknowledgement

The author would like to thank Celia Laverick for providing some of the material included in this book.

Chapter activities

1 Introduction to internal accounting systems and controls

1.1 What is the Internal Accounting Systems and Controls unit designed to help an AAT Level 4 student do? Tick all the appropriate options below.

(a)	Understand the role and responsibilities of the accounting function within an organisation	
(b)	Evaluate internal control systems	
(c)	Enable accountants to find and prevent all fraud	
(d)	Evaluate accounting systems and underpinning procedures	
(e)	Understand the impact of technology on accounting systems	
(f)	Recommend specific accounting software to use in an accounting system	
(g)	Recommend improvements to an organisation's accounting system	

1.2 What information is the scenario and reference material likely to include? Tick all the appropriate options below.

(a)	Company history	
(b)	Recent developments in the company	
(c)	Details of key personnel	
(d)	Set of current financial statements	
(e)	Details of all the accounting systems for the company	

2 The accounting function – how it works

2.1 Who has the statutory duty to ensure a limited company complies with legislation and regulations? Tick the appropriate options below.

(a)	The Managing Director	
(b)	The Finance Director	
(c)	All the directors of the company	
(d)	The company's solicitors	

2.2 Which of the following statements about a centralised organisation is true or false? Tick the correct choice for each statement.

		True	False
(a)	The length of the scalar chain will be shorter		
(b)	Decision making is slower		
(c)	It has fewer levels of management		
(d)	The span of control will be smaller		

2.3 Which of the following statements are true of a wide span of control in an organisation? Tick all that apply.

(a)	Employees can easily suggest improvements to systems	
(b)	It is less expensive to operate	
(c)	Productivity in the organisation will be higher	
(d)	Staff will gain more experience in making decisions	

2.4   You work in the accounts department for a firm of solicitors, Wilson, Patel & Stock. It is run by three partners – Susie Wilson, Priya Patel and Anya Stock – who employ 30 staff. It has two offices – one in Leamington Spa and one in Nuneaton. The business provides services to individuals as well as corporate clients.

   (a)   List the main activities Wilson, Patel & Stock would have to account for and the main accounting functions.

   (b)   What type of structure would you expect Wilson, Patel & Stock to have and why?

2.5   CF Toys Ltd manufactures outdoor toys, including trampolines and climbing frames. The business has several manufacturing divisions, based in different locations across Europe. It employs 450 people. It sells to large toy store chains across Europe and the USA.

   (a)   Identify the main activities CF Toys Limited would have to account for and the main accounting functions.

   (b)   What type of organisational structure would you expect CF Toys Limited to have and why?

2.6   Which regulations will the financial information produced by a limited company need to comply with? Tick all that apply.

(a)	The Finance Act	
(b)	International Accounting Standards	
(c)	The Health and Safety Act	
(d)	The Companies Act	

3 Stakeholders and their information needs

3.1 Outdoors and Active! makes camping equipment including tents, outdoor clothing and sleeping bags. These products are manufactured at three separate factories across the North-East.

The business is owned by four shareholders. The owners founded the business and appointed directors five years ago, when they stopped running it on a day-to-day basis. It has been trading for several years and employs 92 people, most of whom have been with the company for many years. The business operates a productivity bonus system for the employees, paid monthly, based on total production in each factory.

The business supplies products to many independent retailers, as well as two large retail chains, under the 'Outdoors and Active!' brand. It also makes own-brand equipment for both the retail chains.

Most of the products are made using specialist fabrics and parts, sourced from three key suppliers.

(a) Identify the key stakeholders of the business, both internal and external, and explain why they are important. Give examples of information the stakeholders may wish to look at.

(b) Give examples of some possible performance indicators and information to include on budgetary control reports, produced by the management information system, to assist the directors in running the business.

3.2 Polly's Plumbing Ltd is an owner-managed business, run by Polly Green, providing plumbing and heating engineer services, using 20 plumbers and vans. It operates out of an industrial unit and employs four staff who undertake administration, including the accounts information.

Many customers rely on the business to service their heating systems and meet their plumbing needs. The business is particularly good at sourcing parts for older boilers, holding some in inventory, helping clients extend their boiler life. It also fits new heating systems into new-build houses, for a local building business.

The business has recently replaced 10 vans with electric vehicles, obtaining a bank loan for this purpose.

Required:

Identify the key stakeholders of the business, both internal and external, and explain why they are important. Give examples of information the stakeholders may wish to look at.

3.3   EGP Limited manufactures refuse collection equipment. The financial statements are set out below:

Statement of profit or loss for the year ended 31 December 20-6

	£000
Revenue	18,237
Cost of sales	(15,137)
Gross profit	3,100
Operating expenses	(2,735)
Operating profit	365
Finance costs	(45)
Profit before tax	320
Tax	(64)
Profit for the period from continuing operations	256

Statement of financial position at 31 December 20-6

	£000
ASSETS	
Non-current assets	
Property, plant and equipment	654
	654
Current assets	
Inventories	2,613
Trade receivables	1,148
Cash and cash equivalents	707
	5,468
Total assets	6,122
EQUITY AND LIABILITIES	
Equity	
Ordinary share capital (£1 shares)	2,000
Retained earnings	1,956
Total equity	3,956
Non-current liabilities	
Bank loans	500
	500
Current liabilities	
Trade payables	1,617
Tax liabilities	49
	1,666
Total liabilities	2,166
Total equity and liabilities	6,122

Required:

Calculate relevant performance indicator ratios to one decimal place. Include ratios to cover profitability, liquidity and gearing.

3.4   You work for a bicycle manufacturer, which is keen to develop and maintain a reputation for ethical behaviour. You have been asked to review the following policies currently in place to determine if they support ethical and sustainable behaviour or not.

From the policies below, identify if they support ethical and sustainable practices. Tick all that apply.

(a)	All suppliers are paid in accordance with their credit terms	
(b)	Bank reconciliations are produced by qualified staff	
(c)	Customer discounts are determined by the sales director, based on his working relationship with the customer alone	
(d)	Bicycle tyres are sourced from the cheapest supplier	

3.5   Cherie Francis Ltd operates a chain of shops selling accessories, such as scarfs, handbags and jewellery. It leases 90 shops located across the UK and uses an electronic till system to record sales and manage inventory.

From the options below, identify the information that would be suitable or unsuitable for this business to produce for the managers, using its management information system. Tick all options that apply.

		Suitable	Unsuitable
(a)	Profitability by shop vs budget and actual figures on a monthly basis		
(b)	Monthly bank balances		
(c)	Total daily takings for the business		
(d)	Daily staff costs per shop as a percentage of revenue		

3.6   You work as the Financial Controller for a company producing ready meals and report to the Finance Director. They have asked you to reduce the allowance for doubtful receivables from 5% to 2% this month, to improve the profit for the month in the management accounts. These management accounts will be given to the bank, providing the evidence to obtain a bank loan.

When producing this information for the bank, which ethic would you be breaking if you amended the allowance for doubtful receivables?

(a) Confidentiality	
(b) Integrity	
(c) Social equality	
(d) Professional competence and due care	

3.7   You have recently asked for suggestions from the employees in your company to improve ethical and sustainable practices where you work. The company is an established printing company and has been operating for many years, based at the same factory in Plymouth.

Identify which of the following would be a way to improve ethics and sustainability. Tick all options that apply.

(a) Approve a new supplier of paper based solely on which supplier offers the lowest price	
(b) Implement a cycle to work scheme	
(c) Offer training courses to all employees as part of their annual performance review	

3.8   Your colleague has made the following statements about financial information produced by the finance department. Indicate whether the statements are correct or not correct.

	Type of financial information	Correct/Not correct
(a) The statement of profit or loss is used to show the financial performance of the business over a year	Financial	
(b) All budgetary control reports will be distributed to all managers	Management	

4   Internal control systems and fraud

4.1   For each of the weaknesses given below, indicate the cause.

Select causes of weakness from: Lack of leadership, lack of controls, poor implementation of controls, lack of monitoring

(a) There is no policy for sales discounts	
(b) Differences on cash takings are recorded, then not investigated	
(c) Management travel to visit clients three days per week	
(d) The goods returned notes are sequentially numbered manually	

4.2   For each of the controls below, identify whether the internal control is suitable for the purpose given.

Internal control	Purpose	Control suitable – Yes or No?
The payroll software is approved for use by HMRC	Safeguard assets	
Goods received into the warehouse are inspected for quality and completeness	Facilitate operations	
Clocking in and out procedures are overseen by the supervisor	Prevent and detect fraud	

4.3   Ben's BBQs Ltd makes and sells barbeques. It sells to wholesalers and retailers.

The company operates a clocking in system and employees clock in and out unsupervised. The Payroll Clerk sets up new employees on the clocking in system, using information given to them by the employee. The BACS payment for weekly wages is completed and paid by the Financial Controller.

Complete the following statement:

The above may result in the occurrence of [**profit manipulation/misappropriation of money**], that occurs as a result of [**poor implementation of controls /a lack of leadership/a lack of controls**]. To address this fraud risk, the company needs to implement [**a series of physical controls/ reconciliation controls/authorisation controls**] as soon as possible, to minimise the impact on the [**assets/liabilities**].

4.4   You have recently moved from the finance department of a large company to a small one, to improve the internal control systems.   As part of this process, your employer has asked you to identify which internal controls will be most suitable for their business.

Identify which of the following controls are more suitable for either a large or small manufacturing business. Tick the correct column.

Internal control	Small	Large
All purchase orders are authorised by the Managing Director		
The non-current asset register is maintained in a spreadsheet, reconciled periodically to the general ledger		
Bank reconciliations are performed daily using automated software		

4.5   Bumper Beds Ltd is keen to develop a reputation for ethical behaviour. A review of the finance department identified that some of the systems did not currently promote ethical behaviours. You have been given several suggestions to address this.

Identify which of the following would promote ethical behaviours within Bumper Beds Ltd.

Improvement	Promote	Not promote
Introduce a car share scheme, offering incentives to those who participate		
Ensure each director is aware of all passwords of the staff who report to them		
Introduce a staff induction program, including staff policies such as annual leave and use of IT in work		
Introduce flexible working for managers, to allow them to come in later than other employees and leave later		

4.6   Complete the following sentences:

An employee who deliberately scraps finished goods, then takes them home to sell, would be committing the fraud of [**misappropriation of assets/misappropriation of inventory/ misstatement of the financial statements**].

An employee who is claiming personal expenses through their company would be committing the fraud of [**misappropriation of assets/misappropriation of inventory/misstatement of the financial statements**].

An employee who increases the value of closing inventory in the year-end financial statements would be committing the fraud of [**misappropriation of assets/misappropriation of inventory/ misstatement of the financial statements**].

4.7   You have been asked to review the following accounting procedures currently in place in your company. Indicate which procedures include segregation of duties and which do not.

Procedure	Segregation of duties	No segregation of duties
Credit notes and sales invoices are authorised and entered onto the receivables ledger by the Accounts Receivables Clerk		
Purchase orders are authorised by the Production Director. Warehouse staff receive goods into the warehouse		
The cashier opens the post, records customer receipts into the cash book and takes cheques to the bank		

4.8   The Malvern Inn Ltd runs a small hotel in Worcestershire. The hotel is run by a Hotel Manager, who employs several permanent members of staff and uses casual staff over the summer months, to meet high demand.

The reception staff are responsible for checking customers in. The bar and restaurant systems are not integrated with the reception billing system, so any items purchased during their stay are entered manually onto bills by the reception staff, based on the bar till records and restaurant booking information. There are regular customers who visit often and who get to know the permanent reception staff well. The reception staff review the customer's bill, ensuring any meals and drinks are included, prior to the customer settling their account when they leave, and can remove items if they are disputed. There is no reconciliation between the bar and restaurant records and the amounts paid by customers.

The Bar Manager is responsible for ordering all drinks required by the hotel and for counting inventory once every six months. Wastage is not monitored by the accountant. Breakages often happen, along with inventory losses, and the Bar Manager signs off the 'Breakages & loss report', which is filed in the bar. A bar margin report is produced each month, for total drinks sold, and the 'Breakages & loss report' will only be reviewed if the margin appears low.

Required:

(a)   Identify and explain two possible frauds that could occur.

(b)   Grade the risk on the business of each fraud, using the grading system High, Moderate or Low.

(c)   Identify the potential implications of each risk identified.

(d)   For each fraud, identify one safeguard the Hotel Manager could put in place to reduce the risk of the fraud happening.

4.9   Regal Hotels Ltd runs a chain of hotels. It reviewed its activities recently and identified the following potential frauds. There are no controls currently in place to prevent them.

Complete the grading table and a possible control to prevent and/or detect the possible fraud.

Details of possible fraud	Employees	Collusion	Likelihood	Possible control
Inventory Theft of bar inventory	Bar staff	None		
Sales High discounts given to regular customers at the end of their stay in return for payment	Reception	Third party - customers		
Purchases Kitchen staff over-order food, then take it away, recording it as waste	Kitchen	None		

*Grade either high, medium or low

5 Technology and accounting systems

5.1 The accounting software is due to be updated and the managing director has asked you about using cloud accounting.

Identify whether the following statements relating to using cloud accounting are true or false.

Statement	True/False
(a) It allows users to work at home, when necessary	
(b) The accounting software can be accessed, even when the internet is down	
(c) Data is backed up automatically	
(d) Cloud accounting supports sustainability	
(e) Confidential data is held by a third party	

5.2 Complete the following statements:

Machine learning is a type of [**explicit computer programming/artificial intelligence**] that enables an accounting system to automatically update the relevant accounting ledgers, based on the information previously processed.

Machine learning can be particularly useful when combined with [**data analytics/phishing**] to enable users to process large amounts of cost and revenue data quickly.

5.3 You have been investigating data analytics and its application in accounts. Your colleague has asked you to categorise the following tasks in the finance function into the type of data analytic it relates to:

Choose the correct type of data analytic for each of the following tasks. Select the type of data analytic from the following list:

Descriptive, diagnostic, predictive and prescriptive

Task	Data analytic
(a) Forecasting future materials costs	
(b) Reviewing historic trends of material prices	
(c) Using external information to assess a new market	
(d) Production of variances of actual vs budget production costs	

5.4   Complete the following sentences for machine learning and artificial intelligence by choosing the correct option:

Implementing artificial intelligence and machine learning is likely to [**increase/reduce**] staffing levels, [**reduce/increase**] error rates in the inputting of information and have [**high/low**] implementation costs.

5.5   You have been asked to explain to the accounts team the security risks to the accounting data and the operations of the business demonstrated by different circumstances.

Match the correct risk to the circumstances given below.

Select the risk from: phishing, physical loss of equipment, denial of service, data issued in error or unauthorised physical access

Circumstances	Risk
(a) When you click on an attachment from a new customer, the computer screen locks and asks for cryptocurrency to unlock it	
(b) The office alarm code is given to a temporary cleaner, who will clean the office while no one is present	
(c) The password for the payroll system is written in the Payroll Clerk's diary kept on their desk, as they keep forgetting it	
(d) The Payroll Clerk replies to a wages query by an employee using 'All Staff' reply	
(e) A customer has asked for the current bank details using an email address you do not recognise.	

6 Effective accounting systems

6.1 You have been asked to identify policies in the organisation that support ethical standards and sustainable practices. Indicate which of the following policies support these standards and practices and which do not.

Policy	Supports	Does not support
(a) All expense claims are supported by documentation and reviewed by a senior employee prior to being paid		
(b) Employees' salaries are solely determined by the market rate at the time of their employment		
(c) Payslips are emailed to home email addresses		
(d) A staff directory includes home contact details, so the manager can contact an employee if there is an issue on their day off		

6.2 You work for a company purchasing and selling household appliances, such as washing machines, cookers and fridge/freezers. Recently, there have been several inventory losses recorded in the warehouse, so your manager has asked you to set out suitable:

- receiving procedures for purchased appliances being delivered and received into inventory in the warehouse, including updating the inventory and accounting records

- despatch procedures for items being sent to credit customers, including updating the inventory and accounting records

Produce a short report stating the required procedures, including suitable controls, to reduce the likelihood of inventory losses.

6.3 You have been asked to help set up online sales for a clothing company, which has historically sold via two boutiques. The website will allow customers to purchase items that are held in inventory and pay for them using a credit card.

Explain the controls you would expect to be in place for:

- Cash sales in the boutiques

- Sales made via the website

6.4   You work as an assistant accountant for an engineering company, which supplies components to specialist manufacturing companies across the UK. The Receivables Ledger Clerk, who had been working at the business for many years, left suddenly. The Payables Ledger Clerk, Mary, has been promoted to replace the Receivables Ledger Clerk and has been unable to find any written procedures on the raising of invoices. The Finance Director has asked you to email Mary with the procedures that should be in place, as she knows you are studying the AAT Level 4 Professional Diploma in Accounting.

Draft an email to Mary, the Credit Controller, copied to the Finance Director, setting out the invoicing procedures for the receivables ledger. Assume the system is a computerised, integrated system.

6.5   You work at a medium-sized accountancy practice and have just acquired a new client – Johanna's Family Restaurant. The restaurant is due to open next month and Johanna would like to know what she needs to have in place to ensure she pays her weekly paid staff correctly. She has asked your practice to help her complete the weekly paid payroll for the first few weeks, while she recruits a bookkeeper and acquires the appropriate software. She has also set up an employer account with HMRC.

Set out the procedures Johanna should have in place at the restaurant to ensure she pays staff correctly. Payments will be made by Johanna by BACS transfer.

Set out the information she must provide you, to enable your practice to process the weekly payroll and provide payslips.

6.6   Dalton Garages Ltd owns five garages in the South West, repairing and servicing all makes of car. Due to its success, the directors, who all work at one of the garages, have decided to expand and employ managers for a further two sites. A significant amount of non-current assets will need to be purchased to equip each garage, for which the newly recruited managers will be responsible. The directors would like you, as their accountant, to suggest some appropriate procedures over purchasing and controlling these non-current assets.

State the control objectives for purchasing non-current assets. State appropriate procedures for the purchase and control of non-current assets by the newly recruited garage managers.

6.7   You work for a decorating company, Pyle Painters Ltd. The owner, Lilly Pyle, has recently employed an apprentice, who is studying AAT. The apprentice is surprised at how many controls there are in the accounting system and would like you to explain which controls are suitable for certain weaknesses. They have asked you to help them match suitable controls with the following weaknesses.

Select which control is suitable for each of the following weaknesses.

Select from: Segregation of duties, physical access controls, authorisation and approval, competent personnel, check arithmetical accuracy, management controls

(a) Theft of paint from warehouse	
(b) The bank reconciliation has not been performed correctly	
(c) BACS payments can be actioned by the Cashier	
(d) Entry of an inventory loss into the general ledger	
(e) An employee is overpaid due to a calculation error on their overtime	
(f) Sales invoices and customer receipts are entered into the receivables ledger by Receivables Ledger Clerk	

7 Evaluation and review of accounting systems

7.1 Belbroughton Fireplaces Ltd makes fireplaces, selling to retailers on credit. The Operations Director, Sasha Hodgetts, has been streamlining warehouse operations resulting in some space in the warehouse. Several months ago, she suggested the business set up a small showroom and start selling to the public.

The Managing Director, Janice Lee, has asked you to review the sales system in place in the new showroom and sales. The current system is set out below.

The showroom is unlocked and open 9.00am to 5.00pm each day. It is staffed by the warehouse staff, all of whom are trained to help customers that walk in during the day. To get served, the customer rings a bell at the till point, if no staff member is present. Some fireplaces have electric fires in the displays and two fires have been stolen.

Customers who come in either pay in cash or by credit card. There is a till, with a float in, and credit card (PDQ) machine in the showroom. The till is left unmanned for much of the time. A pad of two-part prenumbered invoices is kept by the till for the warehouse staff to complete for the customer. Warehouse staff can give a discount, if needed to secure the sale. When a sale is made, any warehouse staff member will complete the invoice, give a copy to the customer, and record the sale as either cash or credit in the till. All staff have been trained to take credit card payment and several have been shown to do refunds using the PDQ machine, using a common refund code kept in the till.

The staff will take the fireplace from the warehouse and load it into the customer's car.

The Warehouse Manager, Keith, prints the end of day till reports and the PDQ reports each night. This information, along with the copy of the sales invoices, is given to the Finance department weekly, who use it to update the accounts.

Each Friday, the warehouse staff use the sales invoices to update the inventory records.

Required:

(a) Analyse the potential deficiencies in the company's internal controls for showroom sales.

(b) Analyse the cause of the potential deficiencies.

(c) Analyse the impact of the potential deficiencies.

7.2   You work for Playtime for Tots Ltd, a business making toys for children, including educational toys. You have been asked to carry out a review of the sales order processing and your findings are set out below.

Background information

Customers are predominantly UK-based nurseries and playgroups. The business has been working on selling overseas. It has invested in a new website, showcasing its products. Part of the website includes short videos to support the customers, showing them how to use the products most effectively.

The business has invested in sourcing sustainable materials for 100% of its products, along with sustainable packaging. It is keen to promote its green credentials on the website, as it considers this a key selling point.

Sales and orders

The website includes all products and up-to-date inventory levels. Special time-limited offers are tailored to customers, based on their previous buying patterns, to encourage them to place orders. Orders are placed by existing customers either online, using their account, or by phone.

New customers and new products

New customers can only place orders by phone, as there is currently no credit card facility on the website. Customers who would like a credit account must apply, submitting several items of information electronically, which is assessed by the Credit Controller, Sean Walker. Sean determines a suitable credit limit and informs the customer, updating the system.

When customers place an order, the website does not check the customer's credit limit, as the two systems are not linked. Sean reviews if any customers have gone over their limit each day and asks them for payment, stopping any deliveries.

Required:

(a)   Identify **one** strength in the procedures outlined above. Explain how the strength benefits the organisation.

(b)   Identify **one** weakness in the procedures outlined above. Describe the potential damage this weakness could cause the company and a potential remedy.

7.3   First Class Flooring Limited manufactures and sells wooden flooring to independent shops and retailers across the UK. It is based in Woking and employs 150 staff. It produces a range of high-quality products using sustainable wood purchased from 30 suppliers across the globe. The company operates an integrated accounting system, which includes a purchases module. The Production Director, Shelley Plank, is responsible for ordering materials and production. You have been asked to review the adequacy of the purchases and ordering system.

The purchases and ordering system is explained below.

Ordering and receipt

- Production materials are ordered by the stores manager, when he considers the raw materials are running low, using a purchase order.

- Other purchases are made by the departmental managers, using a purchase order number, who order for finance, sales, HR, and marketing.

- Materials are received into the warehouse and inspected. The supplier's delivery note is sent to the accounts department, ready to match against the invoice.

- All other deliveries are made to the department. The departmental manager authorises payment by emailing the accounts department and files the supplier's delivery note with the order.

Posting to the accounts and payment

- Invoices are matched to the delivery note or email from the departmental manager. The price is checked to the purchase order by the Accounts Payable Clerk, Tony Sharp.

- Tony inputs the invoice into the accounts system and authorises it for payment.

- Once a week, suppliers are paid using BACS, authorised by Tony. If the amount of the BACS is higher than £20,000, Tony asks the Financial Controller, Lisa Munroe, to authorise the payment. She reviews the BACS payment listing on her computer, then emails Tony to agree it.

Required:

(a)   Identify weaknesses in the system for purchasing and paying for purchases, outlined above.

(b)   Evaluate the impact that each weakness described in (a) could have on the business.

7.4   You work for Rhona's Jams & Jellies Ltd, which makes batches of preserves and jams. You have been asked to look at the procedures over payroll for casual workers. As part of this process, you have identified the following risks:

- Casual workers have temporarily come from overseas on visas, which are required to work in the UK. Sometimes employment checks are not performed prior to starting work. The visa will give them a National Insurance number.

- The Factory Supervisor can employ casual staff and set the rate of pay for any new member of staff.

- The system for clocking employees in and out using employees' biometric information has been broken for a few weeks. Employees can log in using their employee number. The clocking in and out process has been unsupervised. Overtime payments have risen.

Identify the risks within the system and suggest how you can monitor, review and report on them.

7.5   You have been working on PESTLE analysis for Beautiful Tableware Ltd, a business producing stoneware tableware.

Your colleague, Dylan, is not familiar with PESTLE and has asked you to show which category is appropriate for the statements given below.

Identify the appropriate category for each statement from the PESTLE analysis findings.

	Political	Economic	Social	Technological	Legal	Environmental
Low interest loans will enable investment in new production processes						
New legislation covering disposal of waste						
Tariffs being lowered on exported tableware goods						
Increasing demand of high-quality tableware in overseas markets						
New production machinery to automate the decoration processes						
New suppliers offering sustainably sourced glazes						

8 Recommendations and making changes

8.1 Making Memories Together Ltd is a very large travel company, with a branch in several cities in the UK, which specialises in tailor-made luxury holidays around the world. The accounting system it currently uses was purchased several years ago, when passenger volumes were much lower. The system was an 'off the shelf' purchase. The reservations side of the system is excellent, but the accounts staff input supplier information into a separate purchases ledger, making payments from this, and account for changes in exchange rates using spreadsheets, which is time consuming and prone to error.

Complete the following statements regarding its accounting systems and staff, choosing the appropriate options:

The current accounting system should be **reviewed/replaced/kept the same** as it **is fit for purpose/supports the reservations team/is inefficient.**

A cost-benefit analysis should be undertaken to determine **financial and non-financial factors to consider/only how much a new system might cost/how many accounts staff could be made redundant.**

A new bespoke system **would/would not** be a cost-effective way of improving the current system.

8.2 BL Commercial and Domestic Decoration Limited has been operating for many years, providing decorating services to many different types of clients, including housebuilders, companies and the public. It operates in the Midlands and has one main warehouse.

You have been asked to carry out a review of its purchase order processing, despatch procedures and make recommendations for improvement.

You have interviewed the Purchasing Director (Viktor Popov), Purchasing Manager (Michelle Stone), Finance Director (Rohan Llewellyn), Warehouse Manager (Tau Mosweu) and Accounts Payable Clerk (Lauren Parker). Your findings are below:

Purchase ordering

- Purchase orders for decorating supplies can be made by any of the Contracts Managers, who enter the details into the purchase ordering system, generating a purchase order unique number. Most orders are for a specific sales order.

- Purchase orders quote a customer sales order number, although the purchase order details are not confirmed to the sales order, prior to the order being placed.

- Tau Mosweu, the Warehouse Manager, orders certain standard items to hold in inventory, such as white emulsion and gloss, when he considers inventory is running low.

- Purchase orders are automatically emailed to the supplier.

New suppliers

- Michelle Stone, the Purchasing Manager, works closely with new suppliers, to ensure their products are sustainably and ethically produced. She will go and visit their factory where possible.

- Michelle will deal with negotiating terms with suppliers and aim to negotiate discounts, where possible. She provides all the relevant documentation to a supplier to obtain credit.

- Credit terms are usually 30 days. Any changes to this are suggested and authorised by Michelle.

Receipt procedures

- Orders are received by Tau Mosweu or other warehouse staff, who compares the order to the delivery note. Any warehouse staff member can then authorise receipt of the order, or part-order, in the system. This automatically informs Lauren Parker, the Accounts Payables Clerk, of the delivery.

- The delivery note is filed in date order and held in the warehouse, with a signed copy being sent back to the supplier.

Required:

Make recommendations to the internal controls and procedures of BL Commercial and Domestic Decoration Limited purchase ordering, new suppliers and receipt procedures and explain the benefits to the business.

8.3   Regal Hotels Limited owns a chain of hotels in the Cotswolds. It has been trading very successfully for several years. Its accounts department is based in Broadway, run by the Finance Director. The Operations Directors is also based there.

You have been asked to review the hotel's procedures over staff and make recommendations for improvement.

Background information

Competition for good staff is fierce in the local area, as there is a shortage, so staff are recruited from across the country. To attract staff, the hotels provide staff accommodation on site or nearby. The quality of staff is critical to the reputation of the business, so it pays good wages to enable it to retain staff, once employed. 60% of customers make several visits a year to the hotels, mainly due to the excellent customer service.

Staff employment and training

New staff complete starters forms which are usually approved by the Hotel Manager. The Hotel Manager agrees the rate of pay and the number of shifts, sending this information to Human Resources, who check the paperwork, including identity checks, and ensure it is all in order. The Hotel Manager deploys staff around the Hotel, keeping staff to specific areas – Reception, Bar, Restaurant, Kitchen, etc.

In the summer months, it is very busy and staff sometimes must cover areas they are unfamiliar with. The Restaurant, Bar and Reception Systems are not fully integrated, and Reception Staff must run reports on the computer to update a customer's bill on check out, to ensure all items will be charged for.

The Operations Director has identified several suitable training courses across the business for permanent staff, including for the accounts team. The new courses are run by a local college and start in September, at the end of the busy summer period. Several accounts staff have recently left to further their accounts training elsewhere. This has led to some issues with the accuracy of the accounts, as well as problems with suppliers, due to delayed supplier payments.

Chefs and menu development

The hotels are competing against hotels in their locality. Competitors often employ well known, often Michelin-starred chefs, who produce different tasting menus every few weeks. Regal Hotel Limited's chefs have asked to spend time each month creating new dishes, to maintain their customer base.

Required:

(a) Identify one strength in the procedures within the business, and how it benefits the organisation.

(b) Identify weaknesses in the procedures within the business, the problems they could cause the organisation and make recommendations to resolve them.

(c) Identify one opportunity to improve the procedures outlined above. Explain how the procedure should be changed and how this would benefit the organisation.

(d) Identify one threat to the effectiveness of the procedures outlined above. Explain how the threat could damage the organisation and an action that could improve the risk.

8.4 You are helping your Finance Director prepare for implementing a new purchasing and inventory management system.

Identify whether the following characteristics are associated with phased implementation of a new system.

Characteristic	Associated	Not associated
Different sections of the system are introduced together		
Increased risk of implementation of the purchasing and inventory systems		
Will allow for a change in approach, should it be needed		
Will allow staff to train on each part of the module independently, before moving onto the next		

8.5 Gleam and Glow Ltd is a company making beauty products. The directors have produced a cost-benefit analysis for the wider business and you have been asked to categorise as social, corporate or environmental.

Identify the appropriate category for the following changes:

Suggested change	Social	Corporate	Environmental
Switch vanilla supplier for vanilla body cream to fair trade supplier			
Invest in packaging machinery to improve productivity			
Offer a matched fundraising scheme for employees raising money for local charities			
Convert to 100% compostable packaging			

8.6 Tom's Nurseries Ltd grows plants in four nurseries, to sell in its eight garden centres across the South West. It also supplies garden centres with plants. Its inventory management system is several years old.

You have been asked to review possible new inventory management systems, specific to nurseries. You have spent the last month investigating different systems, incurring costs of £4,500. You have decided the best system is Grow&Track.

The Grow&Track system will use barcodes to track all the inventory in the nurseries. The system will be used to identify how old the plants are, collect materials and labour costs, and log the expected growing time, suggesting dates for despatch to the garden centres. Booking inventory out to customers or the garden centres will be quick and easy, as the staff just scan the barcode of the appropriate items and inventory is automatically updated.

Grow&Track enables the in-house gardeners to see exactly how many of each variety is held and how many days old the plants are. For plants that take longer than a few weeks to grow, such as fruit trees, this is beneficial, as the gardeners must decide which year to sell the tree in to maximise revenue, depending on how good the growing season is each year.

The system is expected to reduce wastage of grown plants by 1.5% per annum. The cost of grown plants last year was £4,300,000.

To implement the system, 12 staff across the nurseries will need to be trained, costing £300 per person. Some of the staff find technology difficult to deal with, as their main job is to successfully produce high quality, robust plants. The Grow&Track software costs £55,000, with additional licensing costs of £10,000 per year.

Nine computers at the nurseries require upgrading for the new software, at a cost of £600 per computer.

The Grow&Track system is expected to deliver inventory holding cost savings of £34,000 per annum.

(a) Complete a cost-benefit analysis for the above proposal, specifying if it is a net cost or benefit.

Costs	£
Benefits	
(Net cost)/benefit	

(b) Identify **four** non-financial factors that should be considered as part of the cost-benefit analysis

(c) Recommend, with two reasons, whether the proposed investment should be made

(d) Identify any factors which would be a concern when implementing a new system.

Answers to chapter activities

1 Introduction to internal accounting systems and controls

1.1

(a)	Understand the role and responsibilities of the accounting function within an organisation		✔
(b)	Evaluate internal control systems		✔
(c)	Enable accountants to find and prevent all fraud		
(d)	Evaluate accounting systems and underpinning procedures		✔
(e)	Understand the impact of technology on accounting systems		
(f)	Recommend specific accounting software to use in an accounting system		
(g)	Recommend improvements to an organisation's accounting system		✔

1.2

(a)	Company history		✔
(b)	Recent developments in the company		✔
(c)	Details of key personnel		✔
(d)	Set of current financial statements		
(e)	Details of all the accounting systems for the company		

2 The accounting function – how it works

2.1

(a)	The Managing Director	
(b)	The Finance Director	
(c)	All the directors of the company	✔
(d)	The company's solicitors	

2.2

		True	False
(a)	The length of the scalar chain will be shorter		✔
(b)	Decision making is slower	✔	
(c)	It has fewer levels of management		✔
(d)	The span of control will be smaller	✔	

2.3

(a)	Employees can easily suggest improvements to systems	
(b)	It is less expensive to operate	✔
(c)	Productivity in the organisation will be higher	
(d)	Staff will gain more experience in making decisions	✔

2.4 **(a)** Invoicing sales, collecting money from customers, paying staff and paying office running costs. The main accounting functions would be payroll, receivables ledger and payables ledger.

(b) A flat structure. As the owners are involved in the business and it has 30 employees, you would expect there to be few layers of management within it. All the staff would probably report to one of the three owners and there would only be few support staff, the main one being the accountant.

2.5 **(a)** Invoicing sales, collecting money from customers, purchasing materials, paying suppliers, recording and managing inventory movements, paying staff and paying factory overhead costs. The main accounting functions would be payroll, receivables ledger, inventory management, payables ledger and bank and cash.

(b) A tall structure. The company is based in several locations and employs a lot of staff. To ensure all operations are controlled sufficiently, there will be several layers of management, based at each location.

2.6

(a)	The Finance Act	✔
(b)	International Accounting Standards	✔
(c)	The Health and Safety Act	
(d)	The Companies Act	✔

3 Stakeholders and their information needs

3.1 **(a)** *Shareholders*

The shareholders are key external stakeholders. They want capital growth for their shares and dividend income from this investment as well.

The shareholders will want to see the annual financial statements to determine the value of their investment and likely future income from dividends.

Customers

The customers are key external stakeholders. The independent retailers will want to be able to offer the Outdoors and Active! brand to their customers. The retail chains will want the business to continue to supply the own-brand equipment.

The customers will want to see the financial statements, to determine the financial stability of the business.

Suppliers

The fabric and parts suppliers are key external stakeholders. They supply the raw materials to go into the camping equipment and want Outdoors and Active! to continue to trade, enabling them to make sales and profits.

Suppliers are likely to have given credit terms to Outdoors and Active! They will require yearly financial accounts to monitor the business's cash flow and ability to repay debts on time, as per the agreed credit terms.

Government

The government is a key external stakeholder, as it wants the business to trade and employ staff, and pay income taxes, company taxes and VAT.

The government will want to see the financial statements to determine the profits generated by the business and so its likely tax revenue.

Employees

The employees are key internal stakeholders. They have worked for the business for several years and are likely to have pensions with it.

The employees are unlikely to have access to the financial accounts. If they work to bonuses, they are likely to want to see weekly and monthly sales figures to allow them to calculate their bonuses.

(b)   The directors are likely to monitor the following:

Performance indicators

- Gross profit margin %, by product
- Operating profit margin % by month
- Inventory holding period (days)
- Trade receivables collection period (days)
- Current ratio
- Acid test (quick ratio)

Budgetary control reports

- Weekly or monthly sales figures by product vs budget and last year
- Monthly sales by customer vs budget and last year
- Materials wastage % (value of wasted material/total material purchased) x 100
- Labour % (labour cost as a percentage of sales) x 100
- Overtime as a % of labour cost (weekly and monthly)
- Level of production bonuses, £ (monthly)

3.2   *Owner/shareholder*

The owner/shareholder, Polly Green, is a key internal stakeholder. She wants the value of her shares to increase as well as to draw an income from the business, either by shares or a salary.

She will want to see monthly management information on revenue and expenses, cash flow and the financial performance of the business.

Customers

The customers are key external stakeholders. The customers have used Polly's Plumbing Ltd for several years and may want to use it to keep their boiler working, rather than replace it. Local builders will want the business to continue so that it can fit the plumbing and heating in its new houses.

Local builders will want to see the financial statements, to determine the financial stability of the business.

Bank

The bank is a key external stakeholder. The bank loan, used to buy new vehicles, needs to be repaid.

The bank will require yearly financial accounts to monitor the business's cash flow and ability to repay debts on time, as per the agreed loan terms.

Government

The government is a key external stakeholder, as it wants the business to trade and employ staff and pay income taxes, company taxes and VAT.

The government will want to see the financial statements to determine the profits generated by the business and so its likely tax revenue.

Employees

The employees are key internal stakeholders. They have worked for the business for several years and will want the business to continue to trade.

The employees are unlikely to have access to the financial accounts. If they work to bonuses, they are likely to want to see weekly and monthly sales figures to allow them to calculate their bonuses.

3.3

Ratio	Formula	Calculation
Gross profit percentage	Gross profit / Revenue x 100 (%)	3,100 / 18,237 x 100 = 17.0%
Operating profit percentage	Operating profit / Revenue x 100 (%)	365 / 18,237 x 100 = 2.0%
Return on capital employed	Operating profit / (Total equity + Non-current liabilities) x 100 (%)	365 / (3,956 + 500) x 100 = 8.2%
Current ratio	Current assets / current liabilities	5,468 / 1,666 = 3.3 : 1
Acid test / Quick ratio	Current assets – Inventories / Current liabilities	5,468 – 2,613 / 1,666 = 1.7 : 1
Gearing	Non-current liabilities / Total equity + Non-current liabilities x 100 (%)	500 / (3,956 + 500) x 100 = 11.2%
Inventory turnover	Cost of sales / Inventories	15,137 / 2,613 = 5.8 times
Inventory holding period (days)	Inventories / Cost of sales x 365	2,613 / 15,137 x 365 = 63.0 days
Trade receivables collection period (days)	Trade receivables / Revenue x 365 (days)	1,148 / 18,237 x 365 = 23 days
Trade payables payment period (days)	Trade payables / Cost of Sales x 365 (days)	1,617 / 15,137 x 365 = 39.0 days

3.4

(a)	All suppliers are paid in accordance with their credit terms	✔
(b)	Bank reconciliations are produced by qualified staff	✔
(c)	Customer discounts are determined by the sales director, based on his working relationship with the customer alone	
(d)	Bicycle tyres are sourced from the cheapest supplier	

3.5

		Suitable	Unsuitable
(a)	Profitability by shop vs budget and actual figures on a monthly basis	✔	
(b)	Monthly bank balances		✔
(c)	Total daily takings for the business		✔
(d)	Daily staff costs per shop as a percentage of revenue	✔	

3.6

(a)	Confidentiality	
(b)	Integrity	✔
(c)	Social equality	
(d)	Professional competence and due care	

3.7

(a)	Approve a new supplier of paper based solely on which supplier offers the lowest price	
(b)	Implement a cycle to work scheme	✔
(c)	Offer training courses to all employees as part of their annual performance review	✔

3.8

		Type of financial information	Correct/Not correct
(a)	The statement of profit or loss is used to show the financial performance of the business over a year	Financial	Correct
(b)	All budgetary control reports will be distributed to all managers	Management	Not correct

4 Internal control systems and fraud

4.1

(a) There is no policy for sales discounts	Lack of controls
(b) Differences on cash takings are recorded, then not investigated	Lack of monitoring
(c) Management travel to visit clients three days per week	Lack of leadership
(d) The goods returned notes are sequentially numbered manually	Poor implementation of controls

4.2

Internal control	Purpose	Control suitable – Yes or No?
The payroll software is approved for use by HMRC	Safeguard assets	No
Goods received into the warehouse are inspected for quality and completeness	Facilitate operations	Yes
Clocking in and out procedures are overseen by the supervisor	Prevent and detect fraud	Yes

4.3 The company operates a clocking in system and employees clock in and out unsupervised. The Payroll Clerk sets up new employees on the clocking in system, using information given to them by the employee. The BACS payment for weekly wages is completed and paid by the Financial Controller.

The above may result in the occurrence of **misappropriation of money**, that occurs because of **a lack of controls**. To address this fraud risk, the company needs to implement **authorisation controls** as soon as possible, to minimise the impact on the **assets**.

4.4

Internal control	Small	Large
All purchase orders are authorised by the Managing Director	✔	
The non-current asset register is maintained in a spreadsheet, reconciled periodically to the general ledger	✔	
Bank reconciliations are performed daily using automated software		✔

4.5

Improvement	Promote	Not promote
Introduce a car share scheme, offering incentives to those who participate	✔	
Ensure each director is aware of all passwords of the staff who report to them		✔
Introduce a staff induction program, including staff policies such as annual leave and use of IT in work	✔	
Introduce flexible working for managers, to allow them to come in later than other employees and leave later		✔

4.6   An employee who deliberately scraps finished goods, then takes them home to sell, would be committing the fraud of **misappropriation of inventory**.

An employee who is claiming personal expenses through their company would be committing the fraud of **misappropriation of assets.**

An employee who increases the value of closing inventory in the year-end financial statements would be committing the fraud of **misstatement of the financial statements**.

4.7

Procedure	Segregation of duties	No segregation of duties
Credit notes and sales invoices are authorised and entered onto the receivables ledger by the Accounts Receivables Clerk		✔
Purchase orders are authorised by the Production Director. Warehouse staff receive goods into the warehouse	✔	
The cashier opens the post, records customer receipts into the cash book and takes cheques to the bank		✔

4.8   **(a)**   **Under-charging of food and drink in return for cash** – Reception staff add on drinks and meals to the customers' bills. They can also remove disputed items. Reception staff could agree to remove meals or drinks with regular customers in exchange for cash.

Theft of drinks – The Bar Manager could take drinks home and sell them, recording them as breakages or inventory losses on the 'Breakages & loss report'.

(b)   *Grading of risk*

Under-charging of food and drink in return for cash

Risk of Fraud – Medium. Reception staff would only be able to do this with regular customers, who could collude with them to commit the fraud.

Theft of drinks

Risk of fraud – High. The Bar Manager knows the 'Breakages & loss report' is not investigated unless the bar margin report is low, so could steal small amounts of drinks often. Any change in bar margin would be unlikely to be challenged.

(c)   *Implications for the business*

Under-charging of food and drink in return for cash

The Hotel Manager would be unlikely to pick this up, as the system is not integrated, so hotel profits would be reduced.

Theft of drinks

If the Bar Manager steals small amounts over a long period of time, it is unlikely to be detected by the Hotel Manager.

(d)   *Safeguards to minimise risk*

Under-charging of food and drink in return for cash – The Hotel Manager should ensure accounts reconcile the food and drinks amounts charged to the bar and restaurant records periodically. Spot checks on customer's bills would also deter reception staff from removing items for customers' bills. Staff rotation would reduce the likelihood of staff and customers colluding.

Theft of drinks – Investigating the 'Breakages & loss report' each week would deter the Bar Manager from committing the fraud. Introducing a till system that recorded inventory and drinks sales individually by product would highlight where losses occurred on drinks. An independent inventory count every month would highlight inventory losses quickly.

4.9

Details of possible fraud	Employees	Collusion	Likelihood	Possible control
Inventory Theft of bar inventory	Bar staff	None	High	Weekly inventory counts and investigation of inventory losses
Sales High discounts given to regular customers at the end of their stay in return for payment	Reception	Third party - customers	Medium	Access to discounts is restricted to specific logins to the Reservations System. All discounts are authorised by the duty manager.
Purchases Kitchen staff over-order food, then take it away, recording it as waste	Kitchen	None	High	Only the Head Chef can authorise purchase orders. Food waste % is monitored and compared across the hotels, to identify any inconsistencies.

5 Technology and accounting systems

5.1

Statement		True/False
(a)	It allows users to work at home, when necessary	True
(b)	The accounting software can be accessed, even when the internet is down	False
(c)	Data is backed up automatically	True
(d)	Cloud accounting supports sustainability	True
(e)	Confidential data is held by a third party	True

5.2   Machine learning is a type of **artificial intelligence** that enables an accounting system to automatically update the relevant accounting ledgers, based on the information previously processed.

Machine learning can be particularly useful when combined with **data analytics** to enable users to process large amounts of cost and revenue data quickly.

5.3

Task		Data analytic
(a)	Forecasting future materials costs	Predictive
(b)	Reviewing historic trends of material prices	Diagnostic
(c)	Using external information to assess a new market	Prescriptive
(d)	Production of variances of actual vs budget production costs	Descriptive

5.4   Implementing artificial intelligence and machine learning is likely to **reduce** staffing levels, **reduce** error rates in the inputting of information and have **high** implementation costs.

5.5

Circumstances		Risk
(a)	When you click on an attachment from a new customer, the computer screen locks and asks for cryptocurrency to unlock it	Denial of service
(b)	The office alarm code is given to a temporary cleaner, who will clean the office while no one is present	Physical loss of equipment
(c)	The password for the payroll system is written in the Payroll Clerk's diary kept on their desk, as they keep forgetting it	Unauthorised physical access
(d)	The Payroll Clerk replies to a wages query by an employee using 'All Staff' reply	Data issued in error
(e)	A customer has asked for the current bank details using an email address you do not recognise.	Phishing

6   Effective accounting systems

6.1

Policy	Supports	Does not support
(a) All expense claims are supported by documentation and reviewed by a senior employee prior to being paid	✔	
(b) Employees' salaries are solely determined by the market rate at the time of their employment		✔
(c) Payslips are emailed to home email addresses	✔	
(d) A staff directory includes home contact details, so the manager can contact an employee if there is an issue on their day off		✔

6.2   Your report should include:

Receiving appliances into the warehouse, including updating inventory and accounting records

- All items should only be accepted if there is a valid purchase order.

- The goods delivery note should be compared with both the physical items and the order for completeness and accuracy. Any short deliveries should be noted on the delivery note, prior to it being signed as evidence of receipt, and a copy returned to the supplier.

- Goods arriving are inspected to ensure they are of satisfactory quality and condition.

- A unique, sequentially numbered goods received note (GRN) is produced for each receipt, detailing the quantity and inventory information for each delivery.

- The GRN automatically updates the general ledger (inventory) and inventory management system for the receipt.

- Once received, items are secured in a locked warehouse.

Despatching appliances from the warehouse, including updating inventory and accounting records

- Only authorised personnel can despatch goods in the warehouse.

- All items should only be despatched with reference to a valid customer order.

- A unique, sequentially numbered goods despatch note (GDN) should be raised, detailing the goods despatched.

- The GDN automatically updates the inventory management system and the general ledger.

6.3 *Controls over cash sales made in the boutiques*

- All cash sales are recorded and stored in a till

- Credit card sales will be recorded separately from cash sales

- Authorised staff (such as the shop manager) counts the cash receipts in the till each day and reconciles them to the till receipts.

- Any differences between cash takings and the till receipts are investigated.

- Where possible, cash is banked the same day, intact.

- If cash is kept overnight, it is stored securely, e.g. in a safe.

Controls over sales made via the website

- Credit card sales via the internet are recorded separately from boutique sales.

- An online payment system is used that authorises the credit payment at point of order.

- Reconciliation of online payments to bank payments, to identify if any chargebacks are made, prior to despatch.

- Comparison of items picked to customer order prior to despatch.

- Confirm customer order is paid for at point of despatch.

- Ensure proof of delivery is obtained by the courier company used to deliver items, in case of disputes with customers.

- Returns process is documented so all returns when received are matched to the customer order and recorded into inventory.

- The return is confirmed as received and back in inventory prior to the customer's credit card being refunded.

6.4

> To: Mary, Credit Controller
>
> Cc: Finance Director
>
> From: Assistant Accountant
>
> **Subject: Invoicing procedures**
>
>
> Dear Mary,
>
> Please see below the procedures that should be in place for raising invoices.
>
> • Raise invoices using the sales order and the delivery note, only once the goods have been despatched.
>
> • The system will automatically give each invoice a unique sequential number.
>
> • Keep any incorrectly issued invoices and file them.   You must not destroy them.
>
> • Agree prices on the invoice to the sales order, including any discount information.
>
> • VAT rates should be verified by you on the invoice, although they are automatically included in the invoicing system.
>
> • Post invoices in batches to the general ledger, which will update the receivables control account.
>
> • Review the receivables control account once the invoice batches have been posted to ensure it reconciles to the receivables ledger balance.
>
> Please let me know if you would like any further information.
>
> Best wishes
>
> Assistant Accountant

6.5   Procedures in place at restaurant to pay staff

- All employees must be issued with a written employment contract detailing rates of pay and contracted hours.

- All personnel records must be stored securely (to comply with Data Protection laws).

- A clocking in and out system, or timesheets, must be maintained to record hours worked. The total hours calculation must be confirmed as arithmetically accurate and also it must be authorised by Johanna.

- Any one-off payments must be authorised by Johanna.

- All employees must provide bank details, which must be stored securely, so Johanna can pay them.

- A standard BACS payment should be set up for staff, with new staff added when needed and staff removed when they leave.

Information required by practice to process payroll and provide payslips

- All starters must have a starter form, approved by Johanna, including:

    - tax code information

    - any previous wages earned (P45)

    - pay rate, including overtime rates

- Weekly hours by employee (clocking in or timesheet) must be authorised by Johanna, including any overtime, and sent to the practice.

- Details of any one-off payments, such as bonuses, must be included.

- Date and details of leavers each week.

- Employer details for the business, given to Johanna by HMRC, so real time information (RTI) reporting can be submitted.

Note: The question asks specifically about staff payments, so payments for deductions, such as PAYE and NIC, are not included in the answer above.

6.6 Control objectives for the approval and purchase of non-current assets

- Only non-current assets that are required by the business are approved.

- Non-current assets are purchased from approved suppliers at the best price.

- Non-current assets are in working order, prior to being paid for.

Procedures over purchase of non-current assets

- The directors approve the capital expenditure budget for each new garage, in detail.

- Only approved suppliers can be used.

- Several quotes are obtained, where possible, to ensure the non-current assets are purchased at the best price.

- Unique, sequential purchase orders are used by the garage manager and approved by the directors for capital expenditure.

- The manager on site thoroughly inspects non-current assets, prior to payment being authorised and made.

Procedures over control of non-current assets

- All non-current assets are recorded in a non-current asset register, in enough detail to be individually and specifically identifiable.

- The non-current assets register will include

    - Purchase date

    - Cost

    - Useful life

    - Depreciation rate and amount charged to date

    - Location

- Periodically, the business should compare the physical items with those recorded in the accounting records (non-current asset register and general ledger), to ensure they are all still held by the company.

- Disposals can only be made by authorised personnel and the non-current asset register will be updated accordingly.

6.7

(a) Theft of paint from warehouse	Physical access controls
(b) The bank reconciliation has not been performed correctly	Competent personnel
(c) BACS payments can be actioned by the Cashier	Authorisation and approval
(d) Entry of an inventory loss into the general ledger	Management controls
(e) An employee is overpaid due to a calculation error on their overtime	Check arithmetical accuracy
(f) Sales invoices and customer receipts are entered into the receivables ledger by Receivables Ledger Clerk	Segregation of duties

7 Evaluation and review of accounting systems

7.1 **(a)** Deficiencies

- No security over showroom
- Till, containing cash, is left unattended
- Cash and credit card takings not reconciled daily to the till and PDQ reports
- Refund information from the PDQ machine is kept in the till
- No written goods received procedure when the sale is made to the customer
- Sales invoice procedures are manual, inefficient, and prone to error
- Discounts can be given to customers by all staff and are not monitored
- Inventory records are not up-to-date

(b) Causes

- Lack of physical controls over showroom access
- Lack of control over till
- Lack of reconciliation of cash and credit card takings to the till report and PDQ machine report
- Lack of control over refunds
- Lack of proof of receipt for accounts
- Sales are recorded on a manual pad and the accounting system updated weekly
- Lack of authorisation of discounts to customers
- Inventory is updated weekly for showroom sales

(c) Impact

- Showroom items have been stolen and damaged
- Cash taking could be stolen
- Cash takings could be incorrect or credit card receipts could be incomplete
- Staff could refund fraudulently to their own credit cards
- Sales could be incorrectly recorded in the accounts
- Discounts could be given fraudulently by staff to friends or in return for cash
- Goods could be stolen and recorded as sold, which would go unnoticed until the end of the week
- Inventory records are not up-to-date, which could result in short orders for credit customers

7.2   **(a)**   **Strength and benefit**

1.   Strength – Up-to-date inventory records.

Benefit - Customers can order knowing items will be despatched shortly.

2.   Strength - Specific targeted promotions for customers.

Benefit - Customers can buy products at a good price, which will encourage higher/more orders.

(b)   **Weakness, damage and remedy**

1.   Weakness – Credit Controller can set any credit limit, with no authorisation.

Damage – Customers may be given high credit limits and subsequently become unable to pay.

Remedy – Authorisation of credit limits over an agreed amount by Finance Director.

2.   Weakness – Website does not automatically check if order is within credit limit.

Damage – Orders may be taken which the customer cannot pay for.

Remedy – Link the website to the sales ordering module to prevent customers going over their credit limit.

7.3   **(a)**   **Weaknesses in the system**

1.   No authorisation limits

2.   Orders are placed based on historic usage not on sales orders

3.   Departmental managers can place orders

4.   Materials, when received, are not matched to the purchase order

5.   No goods received note system is operating

6.   Suppliers' delivery notes are sent to the accounts department

7.   Goods are received by each department

8.   Invoices are input onto the accounts system prior to being authorised

9.   The BACS payment is authorised by the Accounts Payable Clerk alone

10.   The Financial Controller does not review supporting documentation when making a payment

11.   The Accounts Payable Clerk could make payments for over £20,000 and the Financial Controller would be unaware of it

(b)   **Potential impact the weaknesses could have on the organisation**

1.   Raw materials could be ordered unnecessarily

2.   Raw materials may not be ordered for upcoming sales orders

3.   Goods may be ordered by departmental mangers when they are not required, or for personal use

4.   Goods may be received that have not been ordered, so are not required or are incorrect

5.   Goods received not invoiced may not be recorded, so the liabilities will be understated in the financial statements

6.   Suppliers' delivery notes may get lost on the way to accounts. Liabilities due may not be recorded. Disputes will not be identified/will be hard to settle.

7.   Goods delivered to each department may be stolen for personal use but be authorised as payable

8.   Goods may be paid for when they have not been received/be of poor quality

9.   The Accounts Payable Clerk could commit fraud by adding fictitious payments

10.   The Accounts Payables Clerk could commit fraud by making fictitious payments

7.4   Risk – employing staff who do not have the correct visa, so are not eligible to work in the UK

Monitor
- Number of employees found to not have correct visa
- Number of casual workers vs permanent workers

Review
- Internal audit/walk through for starting procedures to identify where more internal controls are required
- Review starter forms, to determine if managers are not undertaking the employment checks

Report
- Use software to highlight new starters with missing information, such as National Insurance numbers.
- Produce chart of casual workers found to not have correct visas

Risk – rates of pay for new staff are not authorised

Monitor
- Rates of pay of new employees
- How much do we spend on casual workers compared with how we anticipated spending

Review
- Internal audit/walk through test to identify areas that need additional controls
- Review new employment contracts to determine appropriate pay rate

Report
- Average hourly rate for casual labour compared to previous year/budget
- Any inconsistent rates of pay for new employees

Risk – staff paid for hours not worked

Monitor

- Average hours per employee vs previous month
- Hours used per batch of jam produced in the factory
- Level of overtime worked

Review

- Internal audit/walk through test to identify areas that need additional controls
- Level of overtime compared with previous month/last year

Report

- Hours paid vs budget
- Inconsistent hours vs previous week or month per employee
- Chart of pay and overtime, highlighting potential excessive overtime

7.5

	Political	Economic	Social	Technological	Legal	Environmental
Low interest loans will enable investment in new production processes		✔				
New legislation covering disposal of waste					✔	
Tariffs being lowered on exported tableware goods	✔					
Increasing demand of high-quality tableware in overseas markets			✔			
New production machinery to automate the decoration processes				✔		
New suppliers offering sustainably sourced glazes						✔

8 Recommendations and making changes

8.1 The current accounting system should be **reviewed** as it **is inefficient.**

A cost-benefit analysis should be undertaken to determine **financial and non-financial factors to consider.**

A new bespoke system **would** be a cost-effective way of improving the current system.

8.2 *Ordering of decorating supplies for specific orders*

The sales order system could be linked to the purchase order to automate the ordering process.

Errors in amounts of ordered decorating items would be removed. It would remove the possibility of over-ordering, which could result in a reduction in cash flow, or under-ordering, which could result in short orders and poor customer service.   It would also remove the possibility of Contracts Managers ordering goods for own use and this going unnoticed.

Orders for holding standard inventory

All orders should be authorised, including those for inventory items.

This would avoid the possibility of placing high value orders, reducing cash flow to the business.

Procedures for using new suppliers

The terms for new suppliers and price negotiation, currently undertaken by the Purchasing Manager, should be supervised and authorised by the Purchasing Director, with input from the Finance Director.

This would avoid the possibility of the Purchasing Manager colluding with suppliers to agree to pay higher prices and pay over shorter terms, then receiving money in return. This would protect the profitability of the business, keeping costs as low as possible.

Match delivery note to order and physical goods prior to receipt

The delivery note should be matched to the purchase order and the goods compared with both, prior to being received by the business. The Warehouse staff should sign the delivery note as evidence of the review, sending an annotated copy back to the supplier and also retaining an annotated copy.

This will avoid receiving goods of poor quality and incorrect items. As the company will have evidence of any delivery issues, it will not pay for goods of unfit quality or missing items.

Goods received note number

A unique goods received note should be generated.

The goods received note should be used as evidence of receipt, and to record any items received not invoiced. Basing a year-end accrual on the goods received notes would ensure the accuracy of the liabilities in the financial statements.

8.3   **(a)**   **Strength and benefit**

Strength – Ability to retain high quality staff due to good wage rates and accommodation.

Benefit – Reduced recruitment costs, good customer service, increased profitability.

(b)   **Weakness, damage and remedy**

1.   Weakness – Hotel Manager can employ staff and set pay rates.

Damage – The Hotel Manager may give higher pay rates to friends who work there or pay more than necessary for particular roles.

Remedy – Authorisation of pay rates centrally by the Operations Director.

2.   Weakness – Staff on Reception may not be trained on billing if the hotel is busy and they normally work elsewhere. The staff may not complete the reports to ensure all items will be included on customers' bills.

Damage – Lost profits due to under-billing for Restaurant and Bar sales.

Remedy – Integrate the Restaurant and Bar systems with the Reception billing system, so any invoice is produced automatically and includes all sales to the customer.

(c)   **Opportunity, change to procedures and benefit**

Opportunity – Offer training courses, run by the local college, to permanent members of accounts staff.

Change to procedures – Introduce a formal training programme for accounts staff, so they are competent in their job and more motivated to stay.

Benefit – Improved relations with suppliers, more accurate financial statements, lower recruitment costs.

(d)   **Threat, damage and remedy**

Threat – Competitors may offer more appealing menus than Regal Hotels Limited.

Damage – Loss of reputation and repeat business, loss of profit.

Remedy – Research menus of hotels nearby. Pay chefs time to develop new menus.

8.4

Characteristic	Associated	Not associated
Different sections of the system are introduced together		✔
Increased risk of implementation of the purchasing and inventory systems		✔
Will allow for a change in approach, should it be needed	✔	
Will allow staff to train on each part of the module independently, before moving onto the next	✔	

8.5

Suggested change	Social	Corporate	Environmental
Switch vanilla supplier for vanilla body cream to fair trade supplier			✔
Invest in packaging machinery to improve productivity		✔	
Offer a matched fundraising scheme for employees raising money for local charities	✔		
Convert to 100% compostable packaging			✔

8.6   (a)

Costs	£
Training for nursery staff (12 x £300)	3,600
IT Equipment (Computers) (9 x £600)	5,400
Software cost	55,000
Licence fee	10,000
Benefits	
Reduction in inventory holding	34,000
Reduced wastage (1.5% x £4,300,000)	64,500
(Net cost)/benefit	24,500
	(benefit)

(b)   •   Gardeners are not comfortable with IT – could they use the system?

     •   Will the new system create any other labour savings?

     •   How will the transition from the old to the new system be managed?

     •   Initially, inventory management will need more time due to the learning curve effect

     •   Better information will improve decision making for management

(c)   Yes the investment should be made, as it will:

     •   Reduce wastage and inventory holding costs

     •   Improve the information for decision making for managers

(d)   The following factors could be a concern when implementing a new system:

     •   Security and integrity of data

     •   Level of preparation of employees

     •   Productivity may decline temporarily

     •   Expectations of users of the system may be unrealistic

Practice assessment 1

The Practice Assessment contains five tasks and you should attempt to complete every task.

Read every task carefully to make sure you understand what is required.

Where the date is relevant, it is given in the task data.

Both minus signs and brackets can be used to indicate negative numbers unless the task instructions state otherwise.

You must use a full stop to indicate a decimal point. For example, write 100.57, not 100,57 or 100 57.

You may use a comma to indicate a number in the thousands, but you don't have to. For example, 10000 and 10,000 are both acceptable.

Scenario

The tasks in the assessment are all based on the scenario of Adams and Blackwall Ltd.

Adams and Blackwall Ltd (ABL) is a heating servicing and maintenance company operating throughout the West Country.

The company is run from a head office on an industrial estate in Exeter and from seven branches throughout the region.

ABL was established in the early 1990s by two of its current directors, James Adams and Hazel Adams (née Blackwall). James and Hazel are majority shareholders. Shares are also held by the other directors and key employees who are encouraged to acquire them through an employee share scheme.

Starting with a single branch in Exeter, the company has grown organically, gradually establishing its branch network throughout the region.

In 20-5 ABL won a contract which involved significant work in the Barnstaple area. This has initially been covered by other branches, but the opening of a branch in Barnstaple was agreed for January 20-6, both to expand the business and to ensure the profitability of the contract.

Developments in the market

Growth in housing associations providing social housing have led to growth in this market. However, competition is keen and margins on tenders can be very tight. During 20-5 ABL lost 2% of its long-term clients in retendering. It gained several new clients during the year and its overall client base has grown by 3% over 20-5. Several housing associations have been through periods of growth and ABL has benefited from this growth. Long-term success is felt to be dependent on both successful retendering to existing clients as well as winning new long-term clients.

Private customers still require repairs and servicing on existing boilers and many have stayed with ABL for several years.

Renewable energy systems have been very much in demand. ABL has invested in MCS accreditation (an industry standard "Microgeneration Certification Scheme"), and also in some staff training in order to be able to compete in this new sector of the market and has seen promising growth in this area.

Resources

In 20-5 the company had revenue of £22 million and employed 370 full-time equivalent employees.

Department	Number of staff
Qualified engineers (including branch managers)	280
Trainee engineers	35
Administration	28
Operations and warehousing	21
Sales and marketing	6

Sustainability

ABL runs an apprenticeship scheme which commonly leads to qualification and employment as an engineer and, overall, staff retention is good.

In 20-5, eight engineers were promoted to senior engineers and the Exeter Senior Engineer was promoted to Operations Director, replacing James Adams, who had previously combined this role with that of Managing Director. All engineers are on the Gas Safety Register and 25% have now completed MCS training (up from 20% in 20-4).

ABL is keen to make savings in waste and energy and take advantage of new technologies, where possible. It is currently investigating initiatives to do so, having started this process by introducing solar panels and an air-source heat pump to heat the offices.

Staff

ABL's key staff are as follows:

Managing Director (MD)	James Adams
Operations Director (OD)	Philip Evans
Sales Director (SD)	Ruby Wentworth
Finance Director (FD)	Richard Johns
Human Resources Director (HRD)	Hazel Adams
Management Accountant	Alex McCrory
Financial Accountant	Kate Brennan
Payroll Clerk	Priti Kumar
Accounts Payable Clerk	Hettie May
Accounts Receivable Clerk	Sanjay Khan
General Ledger Clerk and Cashier	Tonya Ivankiv

All branch managers report to the Operations Director as do the senior engineers.

Task 1

This task is about the purpose, structure and organisation of the accounting function.

(a) You have been asked to review and develop a policy on ethics and sustainability over the next few years.

Identify whether each of the following would be a way to improve ethics and sustainability.

Policy	Would improve	Would not improve
Implement a price increase of 5% for all existing private customers, when costs have increased by 3%		
Introduce speed limiters on vehicles to improve petrol consumption		
Ask all qualified engineers to identify additional training requirements each year		

(b) Identify which of the following is an internal stakeholder.

General public	
Bank, which is tendering for ABL's business	
Shareholders	
Potential employee	

(c) Hayleigh, the Accounts Apprentice, has been learning about performance indicators as part of her course. She has asked you what information is needed from the financial statements to calculate the following performance indicators.

Identify the relevant component required as part of the calculation for each of the following performance indicators. Select from: Revenue, Cost of sales and Equity

Performance indicator	Component required
Inventory holding period (days)	
Gearing	
Trade receivables collection period (days)	

(d) Complete the following statement about stakeholders and the use of financial information by choosing the correct option:

Internal/ external information does not need to comply with accounting standards. If the business is planning to open more branches, the **directors/ bank** will make this type of decision. To monitor this decision, it will use **the statement of profit or loss/ budgeted reports by branch**.

(e) James is considering offering home working, using cloud accounting software, for two days per week to the administration and sales and marketing teams. You have been asked to ensure that appropriate accounting information is kept securely and that data protection regulations are not breached.

Identify whether the following statements relating to moving to remote working and using cloud accounting software are true or false.

Statement	True	False
Cloud accounting will always ensure data is more secure		
Cloud accounting will allow staff from branches and home to access accounting data		
There are no hardware costs when cloud accounting is used		
The use of cloud accounting will ensure malware attacks cannot occur		

(f) You have also been working on the data and operational security policy and the risks the business faces. You have been asked by the Accounts Apprentice, Hayleigh, which the correct risks are for certain circumstances.

Identify the correct risk for each statement below. Select from the following options: Physical loss of equipment, denial of service, data issued in error, unauthorised physical access, phishing.

Statement	Risk
The password for the payroll software is written on a pad by the computer, as Priti, the Payroll Clerk, keeps forgetting it	
Priti is emailing the payslips to staff and this week sends A Hamilton's payslip to A Hamil	
Tonya, the General Ledger Clerk and Cashier, is asked to open a link on an email from the bank's new email address, stating there was a problem with the weekly payroll	

The heating engineers have been issued with tablets, to raise 'on the spot' invoices from private customers. They sometimes leave the tablet in the van overnight	
Sanjay, the Accounts Receivable Clerk, receives an email from a new customer, asking for the bank details in readiness for payment	

(g)   As part of the review of using cloud accounting, James, the Managing Director, has asked you to look at systems that use dashboards and other visualisation methods.

Identify whether doing the following, using the cloud accounting system, would improve or would not improve the financial understanding of managers in ABL.

Statement	Would improve	Would not improve
Presenting accounting information to branch managers using graphs		
Including all the technical terms on any reports produced		
Creating a branch level dashboard showing sales, costs and profit on charts		

(h)   James has also been looking at data analytics and machine learning, as part of the move to cloud accounting, and has asked you whether the following statements about them are true.

Identify whether the following statements about machine learning and data analytics are true or false.

Statement	True/False
A cloud accounting system that uses machine learning to post all entries will be too expensive to buy	
The accounts clerk will not need to code each transaction, using a system with machine learning	
Forecasting will be 100% accurate using data analytics and machine learning	

Task 2

This task is about the types of fraud in the workplace, together with ways to detect it.

James Adams, the Managing Director, is concerned about the suitability of some of the internal controls and he has identified the following weaknesses. He has asked you to explain why these weaknesses may have occurred.

(a) Identify the cause of the following weaknesses. Select from the following options: Lack of controls, poor implementation of controls, lack of monitoring, lack of leadership.

Weakness	Cause
When supplier statement reconciliations are performed, the reconciling items are not followed and investigated	
The non-current assets are rarely inspected and reconciled to the non-current asset register and the general ledger	
The Operations Director is based in Exeter and rarely visits other branches, preferring to hold online meetings with other branch managers	
Engineers can raise invoices, apply discounts to invoices and also take cash payments from customers	

James has recently attended a fraud and anti-money laundering course, hosted by the auditors, and is concerned ABL's procedures may leave it open to these happening. He has asked you to review the procedures over purchases of heating equipment and plumbing parts.

Purchases

ABL purchases heating equipment and parts from several suppliers, who deliver to the branches.

Engineers can call the supplier directly to order boilers or air-source heat pumps, without quoting an order number. If the delivery is for large items, it can be made directly to the customer, or to the branch. Goods are inspected when they are received at the branch or by the engineer when they are delivered to the job site.

When goods are delivered to a housing association site, the site manager will take delivery. As the site managers are busy, they often file the delivery note, expecting the engineer to check the delivery when they arrive on site to install the heating system, which could be a few days later. The deliveries are often made to an unlocked area on site, although the site itself will be locked.

Delivery notes are kept by the engineers and filed at the branch periodically, although they are sometimes lost in transit.

Purchase invoices are sent to the accounts department and entered onto the accounting system by Hettie May, the Accounts Payable Clerk. She will reconcile the accounts payable ledger to supplier statements, for those she receives, and will request copy invoices. She will enter any missing invoice details onto the system before receiving a copy, to ensure the supplier is paid promptly, as late payments have caused issues with suppliers in the past.

(b) Identify two types of fraud that may occur in the above situation. For each type of fraud identified, describe two circumstances that may allow the fraud to occur.

You have recently discovered that The Helpful Housing Association, a major customer, is owned by the brother of Nick Maypole, the Sales Manager.

The Helpful Housing Association buys heating systems from ABL every year. As Nick has worked at ABL for many years, he negotiates the contract price with this customer for its new housing association sites and can authorise any bulk discounts for it.

The Helpful Housing Association has recently requested a particular heating system, EnviroWarm, to be used in its homes and wants ABL to fit these. The heating system is supplied by one supplier, which produces systems at a low cost and only provides a one year warranty. There have been some quality issues with these systems. The Helpful Housing Association has asked ABL to offer a service, parts and labour package for five years, to all new homeowners, at a fixed cost.

(c) **(i)** Identify three potential risks in the system outlined above

(ii) Identify the potential implications of each risk identified

(iii) Recommend an appropriate safeguard to minimise each risk

(d) James is aware that fraud can be either financial or non-financial. He has asked you to identify the categories for the following frauds.

Identify whether the following are an example of financial fraud or non-financial fraud

Example	Financial	Non-financial
Theft of boiler parts by branch staff		
Incorrectly recording apprentice engineers' wages as selling and distribution costs in the financial statements to make the gross profit margin look higher		

Task 3

This task is about the effectiveness of controls.

(a) As the business has grown, the importance of strong internal controls being maintained has been eroded. Richard (Finance Director) has undertaken a review of the current system and identified the following weaknesses. He knows you are studying AAT and has asked you to suggest suitable controls to address the weaknesses.

Identify which control is suitable for each of the following weaknesses. Select from the following options: Segregation of duties, physical access controls, authorisation and approval, check arithmetical accuracy, organisational controls, supervision.

Weakness	Control
The wages control account has been reconciled but the reconciling items not resolved	
The Accounts Receivable Clerk can raise credit notes of any value	
Theft of spare parts from the branch stores	
Engineers can purchase sundry parts, if needed, from local wholesalers in their area	
The General Ledger Clerk and Cashier opens the post and can enter cash receipts and journals onto the cash book	
The wages control account is not reconciled regularly	

(b) Philip (Operations Director) has been on several management training courses since being promoted to director, and is keen to understand whether the internal controls in his area are suitable for the size of ABL, a large organisation.

Identify whether the following internal controls are more suitable for a small or large organisation.

Internal control	Small	Large
Segregation of duties for employing new engineers, entering new employees onto the payroll system, recording hours worked by engineers and making payments to engineers		
Engineers can place orders for any parts required for any value		
The Managing Director signs all cheques and payments		
Production of monthly variance analysis reports by branch		

Task 4

This task is about the monitoring of controls and how they work in practice.

You have been asked to carry out a review of ABL's payroll procedures which are outlined below.

- Branches use a job costing software package called Userve to record and manage jobs that engineers attend. Recording starts with a quote and progresses as actual costs are reported.

- The overall profitability of individual jobs are monitored both at the branch and by Head Office.

- At each branch, engineers submit weekly timesheets to Branch Managers who check information to Userve before signing timesheets to approve them and passing them to a branch clerk for input to Userve. Timesheets are then filed at the branch. Hours recorded are picked up from Userve and input into the payroll software at head office by Priti Kumar, the Payroll Clerk.

- Branch office staff are required to complete weekly timesheets, which are signed by branch managers before being scanned and emailed to head office where details are input into the payroll software by Priti.

- Recruitment of new staff is normally managed by HR at head office, but occasionally a branch manager will employ an additional member of staff on a temporary basis. This is not considered a problem as it mainly relates to cleaners or to engineers required to cover staff sickness on an emergency basis.

- The company uses "Sage Payroll" to perform all payroll processing. Priti is fully trained in this system and the Financial Accountant has completed basic training in it. Access to the system is password protected, Priti has full user rights and Kate Brennan (Financial Accountant) has administrator rights.

- Priti is responsible for inputting all timesheets received before the 25th of each month onto the system and for running the monthly payroll. Employees are paid by BACS on the last working day of the month.

- Payroll prints along with the BACS payment authority are produced by Priti and passed to the Kate for approval. Kate checks that the payroll prints agree to the BACS schedule and that amounts in total are in line with the previous month; significant discrepancies are investigated.

- Back-up copies of payroll data are stored on site in a fireproof safe.

(a)   **(i)**   Identify three weaknesses in the payroll system outlined above

Weakness
1
2
3

(ii)   Evaluate the impact that each of the weaknesses could have on the organisation

Impact on the organisation
1
2
3

You have recently discovered that Hettie May (Accounts Payable Clerk) has been paying a supplier, G May, £3,000 per month, who does not supply ABL with any goods. The supplier's bank details are those of Hettie's brother, George. She has also been overpaying a supplier, LPR Ltd, who Hettie has worked with for many years, by £300 per month for several months.

(b) Identify which of the following procedures would detect the frauds identified above.

Procedure	Would detect	Would not detect
Supplier payments are prepared by Hettie May and checked against the bank payments by Kate Brennan, the Financial Accountant		
Supplier payments are checked for numerical accuracy		
Only the Financial Accountant can set up new suppliers on the BACS payment		
Supplier remittances are emailed to the relevant supplier		
The payables ledger is reviewed by the Financial Accountant periodically and any unmatched cash payments are investigated		
The payables ledger control account is reconciled to the payables ledger each month		

Task 5

This task is about the analysis of internal controls with recommendations to improve them, whilst considering the impact on users.

You have been asked to review ABL's purchasing procedures and to make recommendations for improvement.

The procedures are as follows:

Capital expenditure

ABL's Purchasing Manager is responsible for negotiating all new orders for capital items such as vehicles and equipment. Orders over the value of £1,000 need to be countersigned by one of the directors. The company has a purchase order module in its accounting software which automatically numbers all orders issued and which allows deliveries to be matched against purchase orders by stores and then transmitted to the Purchase Ledger Clerk who matches the received orders against invoices, checks them and passes them for payment.

Plumbing and heating systems and supplies, including microgeneration systems

Parts are ordered by branch engineers, using local suppliers whom the branch manager has agreed prices with. They are charged against the relevant jobs on Userve. Userve does not have a purchase order module but the Purchase Ledger Clerk at head office who receives the invoices can check them against quoted prices recorded on Userve. Branches have built up good relationships with local suppliers over the years and will order from them.

The engineers are often asked to recommend microgeneration systems to replace old boilers. The engineers are trained to gain certification to install these systems, but often choose to recommend one particular type they are used to installing. New microgeneration systems are coming to market every year.

Fuel

The company has an account with BP. Engineers can fill up vans at BP garages and sign for the fuel on the head office account. BP garages use a number plate recognition system so only company vehicles can be refuelled. Head office are sent monthly bills by BP along with a detailed breakdown of fuel usage by vehicle which is used to monitor mileage costs.

Utilities and office supplies

ABL's Purchasing Manager is responsible for negotiating all remaining revenue items using the purchase order system for capital expenditure.

(a) (i) Identify one strength in the procedures. Explain how this strength benefits the organisation.

(ii) Identify one weakness in these procedures. Describe the potential damage this weakness could cause the organisation and suggest a potential remedy.

(iii) Identify one opportunity to improve the procedures. Explain how the procedure should be changed and how this would benefit the organisation.

(iv) Identify one threat to the effectiveness of these procedures. Explain how the threat could damage the business and suggest an action that would reduce the risk.

A cost-benefit analysis has also been produced to support other decisions being made on the continued expansion of ABL. Richard John, the Finance Director, has heard the issues identified can be categorised into Social, Corporate and Environmental. You have been asked to categorise these findings.

The following statements are the results of the cost-benefit analysis.

(b) Identify the appropriate category for each of the following statements.

Statement	Social	Corporate	Environmental
Ability to recycle old plumbing for customers, when it is replaced			
Promotion of renewable heating systems to customers, including loyalty discounts			
Training apprentices in the fitting of renewable heating systems			
Investing in an appointment system, so it can communicate with customers more efficiently			
Reviewing the boilers being purchased to ensure they are built in an ethical and sustainable manner by suppliers			

Richard Johns, the Finance Director, is not familiar with PESTLE and has asked you to show which category is appropriate for the statements below.

(c) Select categories from: Political, Economic, Social, Technological, Legal and Environmental

Statement	Category
More single occupancy housing leading to smaller systems being sold	
The falling pound resulting in higher costs of imported boiler parts, leading to higher servicing prices	
Uncertainties in preferred heating systems due to changing climate change legislation	
Investing in a diagnostic tool that will communicate a boiler fault directly to the company	
Changes to government legislation that requires new fitted boilers to meet certain efficiency criteria	

Practice
assessment 2

The Practice Assessment contains five tasks and you should attempt to complete every task.

Read every task carefully to make sure you understand what is required.

Where the date is relevant, it is given in the task data.

Both minus signs and brackets can be used to indicate negative numbers unless the task instructions state otherwise.

You must use a full stop to indicate a decimal point. For example, write 100.57, not 100,57 or 100 57.

You may use a comma to indicate a number in the thousands, but you don't have to. For example, 10000 and 10,000 are both acceptable.

Scenario

The tasks in the assessment are all based on the scenario of CD Malt Ltd.

CD Malt Ltd (CDM) is a manufacturer of malted grains and malted products mainly for sale to the brewing industry. CDM has expanded rapidly over the last two years. New micro-breweries have increased demand for malt, as well as higher production of low or no alcohol beers. CDM also set up a factory in Southampton, when it moved into producing malted products for the food industry.

Following this period of growth, CDM has asked you, Sophie Miller, an Accounting Technician, to review the processes of the company and identify any weaknesses in the internal controls that may have occurred due to the recent growth of the company.

History

CD Malt Ltd (CDM) was founded in Victorian times, malting grain produced in and around Lincoln. In the 1990s, it was bought by an American conglomerate, then one year ago, it was sold to its UK directors through a management buyout.

CDM is run from an industrial site in Lincolnshire close to the area in which the grains are grown, with a second manufacturing facility in Southampton set up last year. The Lincolnshire site accounts for approximately 2/3rds of its production of malted products. The firm's business is seasonal in that grains need to be purchased at, or shortly after, harvest and then stored until required for production, with consequent impacts on cash flow. Producing malted products for the food industry is a recent development and it has been very successful.

The company employs 120 full-time equivalent employees, 100 of whom work in production and delivery, the remainder in administration.

Recent history

Beer sales in the UK have been in decline for many years resulting in reducing demand. The company had a limited range of products and so has maintained sales by moving into the market for micro-breweries and craft breweries. This has been augmented by increased sales of malt to the EU and to developing economies such as India and Thailand. Moving into malted products for the food industry is a new market and sales so far are increasing each month. Several large food manufacturers have signed supply contracts.

Customers range from multi-national breweries and food producers who buy malt by the tonne, to small micro-breweries who buy 25kg sacks of malt. CDM works hard to know its customers and to provide a high standard of service, and as a result it has a stable customer base. Sales have grown by 6% over the last year.

The firm faces many challenges in the short-term as it begins to operate independently. Management reporting structures need to be redeveloped to suit CDM as a single entity. In addition, CDM has been using systems software developed to suit the group and it is now in the process of implementing the installation of new software across all areas of operations.

The implementation outline, which can be changed if needed, is as follows:

Month 1: Administration, General ledger, Sales invoicing and Receivables ledger

Month 2: Payables ledger, Human resources (and payroll), Inventory

Month 3: Manufacturing, Sales order processing, Purchase order processing

Staff

The directors of CDM are the only shareholders. The key personnel of CDM are listed below.

Managing Director (MD)	Simon Grainger
Production Director (PD)	Katrina Sokolov
Sales Director (SD)	Deborah Jones
Finance Director (FD)	Oliver Matthews
Human Resources Director (HRD)	Jing Cheung
Factory Manager (Southampton)	Mark Widacombe
Production Manager (Lincoln)	Kumar Bhati
Warehousing Manager	Pasha Turan
Management Accountant	Janek Dudek
Financial Accountant	Oti Adeyemi
Assistant Accountant	Susanna Dobson
Accounts Receivable Clerk	Jayne McDonald
Accounts Payable Clerk	Ben Emsley
Payroll Clerk	Paul Arnold
Accounts Assistant (temporary)	Karen Wilber

Sustainability

In the last two years, the Lincolnshire production site benefitted from the updating and upgrading of production facilities improving its capacity to produce the finest grade malts of a consistent quality and improving its carbon footprint at the same time through improved heat reclamation in the drying process (kilning). The production facility at Southampton needs similar levels of investment to improve energy usage.

Both factories use solar power and water collection systems for toilets and office requirements. Any waste products are sold to local animal farmers for animal feed. CDM works with local farmers, who operate sustainably, many of whom are also organic.

Task 1

This task is about the purpose, structure and organisation of the accounting function.

Karen Wilber, the temporary Accounts Assistant, is studying AAT and has commented that CDM runs it operations in a centralised manner. She would like to know if the following statements about a centralised structure are true or false.

(a) Identify whether the following statements about a centralised structure are true or false.

Statement	True/ False
Decision making will be faster, as the length of scalar chain is shorter	
The span of control is likely to be narrow	
Productivity will be higher	
It is more expensive to operate	

CDM produces different types of financial information for its stakeholders.

(b) Complete the following statements:

Financial information produced for **internal/external/all** stakeholders must **always/often/ sometimes** be produced using ethical principles.

External stakeholders will expect financial statements to **comply/not comply** with the conceptual framework and accounting standards. This will allow stakeholders, such as the bank, to make informed decisions on **loans applications/buying shares** that will enable the business to grow.

(c) Identify whether the following statements about financial information are correct or incorrect.

Statement	Type of financial information	Correct/Incorrect
The statement of cash flows is useful to the bank, to monitor whether CDM can repay its loans	Financial	
The budgetary control reports are used to determine the overall profitability of the organisation	Management	

The new systems due to be implemented include some elements of machine learning and data analytics.

(d)   Identify whether the following statements about machine learning and data analytics are true or false.

Statement	True/False
Machine learning and data analytics cannot be used in the same parts of the accounting system	
Data analytics can be useful audit tools	
Using a system including machine learning and data analytics will de-skill the accounting staff	
Data analytics could be used to predict future grain costs	
Machine learning will result in less inaccurate information due to coding errors	
Machine learning and data analytics can be used on multiple sites	

The new accounting systems include data dashboards, to summarise key data in each accounting system.

(e)   Identify whether the following statements relating to visualisation, including data dashboards, are true or false.

Statement	True/False
Data dashboards will always make information more understandable to non-financial managers	
Graphs are a key visualisation tool on a data dashboard	
Dashboards can include performance indicators	
Data dashboards are designed to meet non-financial users' needs	

The directors at CDM have been considering whether to implement a flexible 'work from home' policy for non-production staff. You have been asked to review the policy to protect CDM's data and assets.

(f)   Identify which of the following are required to protect company data and equipment when working from home.

Statement	Required	Not required
Virus protection must be enabled and users cannot disable it		
Data stored on a laptop is suitably encrypted		
The laptop must be stored in a locked cupboard overnight		
Passwords must be changed regularly and not shared		
The screen lock must be enabled at all times while the computer is unattended		

Task 2

This task is about the types of fraud in the workplace, combined with ways in which it can be detected and prevented.

CDM pays its production workers weekly. The production workers clock in and out each day, using a card system. The factory supervisor trusts the staff to clock in and out correctly.

The clocking in information is sent to Paul Arnold, the Payroll Clerk, who uses the information to automatically update the payroll software. Paul can amend the hours on the payroll, if needed. The gross pay report is generated and Oti Adeyemi, the Financial Accountant, reviews this periodically.

The employees are paid by BACS transfer each Friday by Oti.

(a)   Complete the following statements:

The above may result in the occurrence of **monetary/inventory** fraud, that could occur as a result of **a lack of controls/poor implementation of controls/a lack of monitoring.**

In order to address this risk, you may need to implement **physical controls/segregation of duties/authorisation and approval** as soon as possible. This will ensure the impact on **liabilities/income/assets** is minimised.

The Southampton factory is run by the Mark Widacombe, the Factory Manager. The Production Director, Katrina Sokolov, lives in Lincoln, so only visits the Southampton factory when there are production issues. A non-current asset register is maintained for both sites. The non-current asset register and the general ledger are reconciled at the year-end.

To comply with specific customer and product requirements, the factory often buys new pieces of equipment. Mark can place orders for equipment as needed. He will deal with the supplier and agree the price of the equipment. The factory hours are 8.00am until 5.00pm, and as deliveries sometimes come early, Mark often goes in early to receive these goods.

Non-current assets are counted once a year and if non-current assets are found to be missing, they are removed from the register and written out of the general ledger. Katrina would like to implement a system using unique bar codes on non-current assets, to make counting and reconciling the non-current assets more efficient, but Mark has been too busy to implement it.

Some equipment and vehicles were transferred from Lincoln when the factory was set up and Mark is responsible for deciding when to sell old equipment and vehicles. He will find a buyer and determine an acceptable price. A miscellaneous sales invoice is raised and Mark informs Susanna Dobson, the Assistant Accountant. She then removes the asset from the non-current asset register and the general ledger.

(b)   **(i)**   Identify four weaknesses in the system that may result in a fraud occurring

(ii)   Recommend an internal control for each weakness, giving a reason why it will prevent fraud

Weakness that may result in fraud	Internal control to prevent fraud and reason

Oliver Matthews, the Finance Director, has recently identified a number of areas where he feels fraud may be possible. He knows you are studying AAT and would like you to complete the fraud matrix for him.

(c)   Identify the appropriate rating for each of the situations given below. Select from: Low, Medium, High

Situation	Rating
CDM uses weighbridges to weigh vehicles on arrival with a full load and then vehicles are weighed again on departure to calculate the weight of grain delivered. Copies of weighbridge results are passed to farmers. Purchase invoices are completed using price lists and weighbridge documentation by CDM and sent to the farmer for approval of price and weight.	
Jayne Dudek, the Management Accountant, produces the monthly management accounts. She enters journals to the general ledger, along with Oliver Matthews, the Finance Director.	
Each day the post is opened by two people, who record all cash receipts. These are entered into the cash book by Susanna Dobson, the Assistant Accountant, which automatically updates the receivables ledger.	

You have been reviewing the sales ordering and invoicing procedures with Deborah Jones, the Sales Director and Jayne McDonald, the Accounts Receivable Clerk. You have identified the following risks in the system:

- Urgent orders placed by customers will be despatched the same day. Sometimes the sales staff do not check the credit limit prior to the order being accepted.

- When a customer queries an invoice, the Accounts Receivable Clerk, Jayne McDonald, can issue a credit note for up to £500 to resolve the problem.

- Sales prices are agreed by the customer and the relevant Sales Manager, who can give discounts of up to 10% if they feel it appropriate. These are not authorised by the Sales Director, Deborah Jones.

(d) Outline how you can monitor, review and report on one of the risks in the system above.

Risk
Monitor
Review
Report

Task 3

This task is about the effectiveness of controls.

The temporary Accounts Assistant, Karen Wilber, who is studying AAT, is currently learning about internal controls. She has asked you to review the following internal controls, to see if they are suitable for the purpose given.

(a)   Identify whether the following internal controls are suitable for the purpose given.

Internal Control	Purpose	Suitable – Yes/No
Regularly reconcile the VAT control account	Prevent and detect fraud and error	
The directors are the only authorised signatories on the bank accounts	Compliance	
Monthly management accounts are produced and reviewed	Safeguard assets	
The new accounting system is cloud based and is backed up automatically	Facilitate operations	

CDM's customers usually buy on credit, but some customers buy in cash direct from the warehouse. You have been asked by Deborah Jones, the Sales Director, whether the following controls for a sales ordering system are appropriate for cash-based, credit-based or online transactions.

(b)   Identify whether the following controls are more suitable for cash-based, credit-based or online transactions.

Internal control	Cash-based	Credit-based	Online
Customers are subject to rigorous credit checks with a credit agency prior to orders being placed			
Payment is made prior to the order being confirmed and delivery details being obtained			
Customers pay for the goods at point of order and collection			

CDM is keen to support sustainable practices as many customers now wish to purchase sustainably produced ingredients. Following a review of the accounting department, some practices have been identified that promoted unsustainable practices. You have been given the following improvements to address this.

(c)   Identify which of the following would promote sustainable behaviours within CDM.

Improvement	Would promote	Would not promote
Employees with hybrid or electric cars are given priority parking		
All non-grain suppliers are chosen solely based on lowest price		
All new starters complete an induction programme		

Task 4

This task is about the monitoring of accounting systems and how they work in practice.

You have been asked to carry out a review of CDM's proposed receivables ledger procedures which are outlined below.

In month 1 the invoicing and receivables ledger module of the new IT system goes live. However, the sales order processing module, which will link to it, does not go live until month 3. As a result, temporary procedures have been introduced to be used for the interim period when there will be no automatic updates from the sales team or despatch departments to the accounting system.

Ordering and despatch

- Sales staff will be responsible for pricing customers' orders received using an Excel spreadsheet produced for that purpose. A new worksheet will be used for each order.

- Sales staff will be able to view customers' accounts on the IT system and will check their status and credit limits before accepting orders. Once an order is accepted, they will print a copy of the worksheet, post it to the customer and email one copy of the worksheet to production and another copy to Jayne McDonald, the Accounts Receivables Clerk.

- Production schedules will be planned around customers' orders and once goods are ready for shipping, the order worksheets will be emailed to despatch.

- Once goods are despatched, the worksheet is updated to show despatch details and emailed to Jayne McDonald.

Accounting

- Jayne MacDonald is to raise invoices on the basis of worksheets received from despatch. These will be priced automatically by the new software, including VAT where appropriate, and will state the agreed terms of sale and be emailed to the customers.

- Customer queries regarding orders and receipts are directed initially to the sales team. If a credit note is required to solve a problem, the Sales Manager will email Jayne McDonald asking for a credit note to be raised and explaining why this is necessary.

- Customers' statements are run at the month end on the new software and emailed to customers.

- Susanna Dobson, the Assistant Accountant, will reconcile the total of the receivables ledger balances to the receivables ledger control account at the month end.

(a) Using the form on the next page, identify the potential deficiencies in CDM's proposed internal controls for sales accounting, together with their cause and impact.

Deficiencies

Causes

Impact

(b)   Identify whether the following statements are true or false.

Statement	True/False
The most expensive accounting system will always be the best	
Electronic invoicing is more cost effective than paper-based invoicing	
Qualified accounting staff should help CDM support ethical principles	

(c)   When the new factory was purchased in Southampton, several new staff joined the company. CDM requires all staff to attend induction training, as well as subsequent training to ensure internal controls operate effectively.

Complete the following statement:

The accounting system must be **reviewed regularly/updated yearly** to ensure it **meets the needs of the organisation/can be used by all staff.**

Task 5

This task is about the analysis of internal controls, with recommendations to improve whilst considering the impact on users.

You have been asked to review a new forecasting system for grain purchase planning. The current system operates as follows:

Current Grain Purchase forecasting and planning procedures

Deborah Jones and Katrina Sokolov, the Sales and Production Directors respectively, meet in the run up to harvest to decide on expected sales volumes by category of malt for the coming year. This will feed into plans for the quantity of purchases. Oliver Matthews, the Finance Director, is involved at this point as he will need to make sure that the firm can finance the level of purchases required.

Once plans are agreed, CDM's two buyers will be informed, and they will work to achieve the planned levels of purchases. To improve the reliability and quality of supplies, CDM agrees long term contracts with farmers who sell the grains. The contracts are fixed price contracts for three years – CDM gets guaranteed supply and the farmers get a guaranteed price, dependant on quality. Approximately 50% of supply is covered by these agreements. The remainder is bought on the open market and can be imported if required, although this is usually more expensive.

New Grain Purchase forecasting and planning system

You have been investigating several software packages to help with grain forecasting and have identified a suitable new package, GrainStore. The research costs to date are £3,600. The existing grain contracts would need loading onto the new system, at a cost of £6,000.

Deborah Jones, Katrina Sokolov and Oliver Matthews would all need to attend a two-day training course, costing £1,600 per day. You would also need to attend the course. The two buyers would need to attend a one-day course for £800 each.

The software licence costs £15,000 per annum and some hardware upgrades would be required, costing £17,500.

This year, CDM expects to purchase grain costing £12.4 million. Improving the forecasting and buying of grain, is expected to save 0.5% of the total grain costs. Overtime totalling £3,000, paid to the buyers, will also be saved. The buyers have received this payment for several years.

The reporting of information is far more extensive then the current system.

(a) **(i)** Complete a financial cost-benefit analysis for the above proposal, specifying if it is a net cost or benefit.

Costs	£
(Net cost)/ benefit	

(ii) Identify six non-financial factors that should be taken into account as part of the cost-benefit analysis.

(iii) Recommend, with two reasons, whether or not the proposed investment should be made.

(b) When implementing a new system, which of the following would be a significant concern to management? Tick all options that apply.

Concern	Yes/No
Data could be lost or transferred incorrectly	
The old system may be used for longer than expected	
Controls may not operate effectively	
Ethical principles may be breached	
The service to customers or suppliers may be adversely affected	
Staff may become demotivated	

You are now considering the new accounting system. As part of the new system's implementation, you have been looking at how to ensure it is successful.

(c) Identify whether the following characteristics are associated with a phased implementation, the approach adopted by CDM.

Characteristic	Associated / Not associated
Staff may be overwhelmed with changes	
Staff will determine when the next phase is implemented	
Data will be transferred between the old and new systems	
Will reduce staff productivity temporarily	
Risk of data corruption is increased	
Higher costs due to inputting information twice	

Practice assessment 3

The Practice Assessment contains five tasks and you should attempt to complete every task.

Read every task carefully to make sure you understand what is required.

Where the date is relevant, it is given in the task data.

Both minus signs and brackets can be used to indicate negative numbers unless the task instructions state otherwise.

You must use a full stop to indicate a decimal point. For example, write 100.57, not 100,57 or 100 57.

You may use a comma to indicate a number in the thousands, but you don't have to. For example, 10000 and 10,000 are both acceptable.

Scenario and reference material

Scenario

Company background and history

The Fabled Baker Limited (FBL) is a food manufacturer which runs a chain of bakeries operating in the Midlands. The company owns a factory which produces the majority of the items which are sold in its shops. The company's head office is based with its factory on an industrial estate in Coventry.

The company was started by master baker Peter Taylor and his wife Jean who set up a single bakers' shop in Tamworth thirty years ago. The firm expanded over the years under the management of their children and by 20-0 had become a limited company owned and managed by the Taylor family with over 80 high street shops. At this point the factory was built and instore bakeries closed. The management of the firm moved to Coventry and consolidated operations as a regional bakery network.

The firm continued to expand, although at a slower rate, until the start of the recession in 20-8. Margins had always been tight due to supermarket competition, but this had been offset by sales volume – which fell dramatically in 20-8. Management's response has been to close some shops and to move more clearly into the food-on-the-go market. This has seen the company move back into profitability. The majority of shares in FBL are still owned by the Taylor family, but the current Sales, Production and Finance Directors each have a 10% stake in the company.

In 20-9 FBL had revenue of £42 million, an increase of 3% over 20-8, and employs 924 employees. It is split into two divisions:

- Retail – 675 employees, working in 73 shops

- Production – 210 employees working the factory and distribution and the remainder in Product Development, Administration and Finance.

Mission statement

The Fabled Baker Limited aims to live up to its name, providing high quality and memorable food to all its customers with outstanding levels of customer service.

The firm is, at its core, a family business deeply rooted in the Midlands with a strong work ethic and high degree of loyalty to staff, customers and local communities.

Developments in the market

The trend in declining sales of traditional bakery products such as loaves of bread continues. Alongside this there is significant growth in the market for food-on-the-go. Demand for sandwiches, for savouries such as sausage rolls and pasties, as well as for biscuits and cakes continues to grow. FBL has tried to move its business into the food-on-the-go market by developing new products, such as a breakfast range, and a range of fresh soups. The success of the range of soups has been such that FBL has, for the first time in 20-9, been able to sell these to several supermarket chains for sale in their chilled food sections. The credit sales of soup accounted for 3% of total sales in 20-9. FBL has also invested in coffee machines for its shops and opened a small number of new shops in areas where many people work but where there are few shops.

Several high streets and town centres continue to struggle with the changing demand arising from out-of-town shopping centres and the rise of online shopping. FBL only closed shops with reluctance in the past and still has several stores which are generating very low profits.

FBL has always paid staff above the minimum wage and so increases in this do not directly affect it, but staff costs in 20-9 rose by 5% as wage rates were increased to maintain pay differentials. Raw materials prices also rose.

Strategic planning

The company uses the balanced scorecard to assess its overall performance.

Learning and growth

FBL employs a well-qualified product development team at its factory. They are responsible for constantly reviewing and renewing the firm's product range in line with changing consumer tastes. In 20-9, 20% of product lines were "refreshed" and like-for-like sales responded with growth of 8%. In addition, 56 new products were added to the firm's product portfolio over the year. In week 52, 12% of sales were from product lines launched in 20-9. Training requirements of established and of new staff are carefully reviewed and staff regularly attend training sessions at head office – such as in the use of the barista coffee machines.

Business processes

In 20-9 the firm upgraded one production line at its factory and invested in a new soup making production facility. This investment, along with the refurbishment of eight shops and the investment in new equipment at all shops, combines to increase the capacity of the firm to meet its customers' needs.

Customers

Customer satisfaction is monitored through performance indicators measuring both footfall and average spend per customer in each shop. Both indicators showed positive growth in 20-9. In addition, regular customer satisfaction surveys are carried out, and at the end of 20-9 these show that customers see the firm as offering high quality products and friendly service which is good value for money.

Financial

Revenue grew by 3% in 20-9 and the firm achieved a ROCE of 13%, up from 12% in 20-8. The Taylor family is happy with this improvement, but the three directors are keen to see the company further improve its financial results. They argue that with the level of uncertainty faced by the economy in general, FBL needs to make more decisions based on purely financial factors, and in particular to seriously consider closing or re-developing marginally profitable shops.

Staff

FBL's employees responsible for the strategy of the firm overall are:

Managing Director (MD)	Robert Taylor
Production Director (PD)	Brian Stead
Sales Director (SD)	Elaine Anderson
Finance Director (FD)	Alison Davis
Human Resources Director (HRD)	Sanjeev Grover
Management Accountant	Will Dodds
Assistant Accountant	Vikki Weatherby
Accounts Payable Supervisor	Suri Salam
Accounts Receivable Clerk	Chris Robins
General Accounts Clerk	Mo Taylor
Payroll Manager	Anya Kolowski

The Finance Director produces FBL's annual statutory accounts and is responsible for all finance, legal and IT issues.

Task 1

This task is about the purpose, structure and organisation of the accounting function.

(a)   You have been asked to review and develop a policy on ethics and sustainability over the next few years.

Identify whether each of the following would be a way to improve ethics and sustainability.

	Would improve	Would not improve
Give unsold food to local hostels and food banks		
Set a target to employ at least one apprentice at every location within the next two years		
Implement productivity bonuses on evening production shifts only		

(b)   Identify which of the following is an internal stakeholder.

Customers	
Bank	
Employee	
Suppliers	

(c)   Mo Taylor, the General Ledger Accounts Clerk, has been learning about performance indicators as part of his AAT course. He has asked you what information is needed from the financial statements to calculate the following performance indicators.

Identify the relevant component required as part of the calculation for each of the following performance indicators. Using each option only once, select from: Operating profit, cost of sales, current liabilities, and inventories.

Performance indicator	Component required
Quick (acid test) ratio	
Return on capital employed	
Current ratio	
Trade payables collection period (days)	

(d) Alison Davis, the Finance Director, is considering using data analytics in FBL. She has asked you to match the type of data analytic to the most suitable suggested purpose.

Match the purpose with the most appropriate type of data analytic. Using each option only once, select from: Descriptive, diagnostic, prescriptive, predictive.

Purpose	Type of data analytic
Produce budgetary reports of budget to actual information	
Recommend new types of products to make and sell, based on internal and external research	
Find the reason for adverse production variances	
Forecast sales by product type	

(e) Alison Davis, the Finance Director, is also considering implementing some new accounting software. She has asked you to review the budgetary control information currently given to the non-financial managers in the business, considering if the new accounting software could improve the understanding of it by non-financial managers.

Complete the following sentences by choosing the correct option:

Budgetary control information may be more easily understood by shop and production managers if it is presented **in a table/using a data dashboard.** Non-financial managers may require information presented **in a clear, uncluttered format/using interactive drill-down menus and charts.**

To ensure the information is understandable, you should **include a glossary of key terms/discuss it with managers with limited financial knowledge.**

(f) Robert Taylor, the Managing Director, is interested to know how a new cloud accounting system might affect the accounts team and the rest of the business.

Identify whether the following statements relating to implementing cloud accounting are true or false.

Statement	True/False
Cloud accounting is not compatible with data analytics	
Cloud accounting will result in higher hardware costs	
Staff productivity is unlikely to be affected, if remote access is stable and reliable	
Data is backed up automatically, resulting in less likelihood of data loss	
Cloud accounting includes machine learning, which reduces errors	

(g) You have also been working on the data and operational security policy and the risks the business faces. You have been asked by the Assistant Accountant, Vikki Weatherby, which the correct risks are for certain circumstances.

Identify the correct risk for each statement below. Select from the following options: Physical loss of equipment, denial of service, data issued in error, unauthorised physical access, phishing

Statement	Risk
Anya Kolowski, the Payroll Manager, emailed A Jones's payslip to B Jones	
The Production Manager has shared his password with the Factory Supervisor, to enable production to operate efficiently	
Mo Taylor, the General Accounts Clerk, receives an email from the bank, asking him to click on a link to confirm the bank details for a BACS payment	
Shop managers use laptops during the day. The laptop is left unattended on the desk at the back of the shop office	

Task 2

This task is about the types of fraud in the workplace, combined with ways in which it can be detected and prevented.

Robert Taylor, the Managing Director, is concerned about the suitability of some of the internal controls and he has identified the following weaknesses. He has asked you to explain why these weaknesses may have occurred.

(a) Identify the cause of the following weaknesses. Select from the following options: Lack of controls, poor implementation of controls, lack of monitoring, lack of leadership

Weakness	Cause
Management and supervision of shops is often remote	
There is no limit on the amount the Production Manager can order from suppliers of raw materials	
The Production Director infrequently investigates the materials usage and labour utilisation variances in the factory	
When the VAT return is completed and reconciled to the VAT control account, reconciling items are not followed and cleared	

Robert has recently attended a fraud course, hosted by the auditors, and is concerned FBL's procedures may leave it open to fraud. He has asked you to review the following procedures over purchases of inventory for the factory and products sold in the shops, such as drinks and crisps.

Purchases – factory ingredients

FBL purchases ingredients from a few suppliers, some of whom have been used for several years.

The Production Manager places orders for ingredients for the factory every day, based on planned production. He often phones the supplier to place the order, quoting the order number, and agreeing the price. As some ingredients are seasonal, prices can vary considerably from week to week. The order is then emailed to the supplier.

Goods are delivered to the factory and received by the warehouse staff, who check the delivery note back to the purchase order. All delivery notes are sent to the Production Manager, who reviews them for any discrepancies, then sends them to Suri Salam, the Accounts Payable Supervisor. One of the Accounts Payable team uses the delivery note to update the purchases systems to show which items have been delivered.

Purchases - ancillary shop products

Shop managers can order ancillary shop products, such as drinks and crisps, as needed by phone, using the specific suppliers at prices agreed by Elaine Anderson, the Sales Director. A numbered purchase order is issued at this point.

Orders are received by the Shop Manager, who signs the delivery note as proof of delivery. The delivery note is then scanned and sent to the relevant Accounts Payable Clerk in the accounts department, ready to match with the purchase order and invoice. The inventory is stored in an unlocked area at the back of the shop until needed.

Purchases – accounts department

Purchase invoices are sent to the accounts department and entered onto the accounting system by a member of Suri Salam's team. Purchase invoices will be electronically matched to the purchase order. Any discrepancies for factory items will be sent to the Production Manager to investigate; any discrepancies with shop items will be sent to the relevant Shop Manager. The Production Manager can authorise payment of an invoice where there is a discrepancy. Shop managers can also authorise payment, even where there are any discrepancies. This is to avoid any supply issues with the suppliers.

Inventory count

Periodically, the value of shop inventory is estimated by the Shop Manager, so a profit or loss by shop can be completed. This is an estimate and is not detailed item by item. The shop inventory held is considered of low value.

(b) Identify two types of fraud that may occur in the above situation. For each type of fraud identified, describe two circumstances that may allow the fraud to occur.

You have been asked to review some of the procedures in the shops.

FBL employs many part-time staff in the shops and has a high staff turnover. The till system is complex to use and staff need training to ensure they operate the till correctly. Factory production is determined using the combined sales information from the tills in the shops.

The tills are connected to the internet and are used to process credit card payments, as well as store cash. Sometimes, the internet connection in the shop is interrupted and the credit card function does not work, so the shop must revert to 'cash only'. Customers do not always carry the cash to pay for items.

Many shop employees work hours that include an unpaid break. Some shop managers make the employees work the unpaid break, but do not amend the hours paid to the employee to allow for this.

(c) **(i)** Identify three potential risks in the system outlined above

(ii) Identify the potential implications of each risk identified

(iii) Recommend an appropriate safeguard to minimise each risk

(d) Robert is aware that fraud can be either financial or non-financial. He has asked you to identify the categories for the following frauds.

Identify whether the following are an example of financial fraud or non-financial fraud

Example	Financial	Non-financial
Stealing cash takings from the till in the shop		
Adjusting the depreciation rates on non-current assets so the depreciation charge is lower in the year, overstating profits, to earn a company-wide staff bonus		

Task 3

This task is about the effectiveness of controls.

(a)   As the business has grown, the importance of strong internal controls being maintained has been eroded. Alison Davis, the Finance Director, has undertaken a review of the current system and identified the following weaknesses. She knows you are studying AAT and has asked you to suggest suitable controls to address the weaknesses.

Identify which control is suitable for each of the following weaknesses. Select from the following options: Segregation of duties, physical access controls, authorisation and approval, check arithmetical accuracy, personnel, management

Weakness	Control
Bank reconciliations are produced by Mo Taylor, the General Accounts Clerk, who is unqualified	
The Accounts Payables Supervisor, Suri Salam, posts purchase invoices and payments to the payables ledger	
The payroll computer is kept in an unlocked office	
Casual production staff are employed by the Factory Supervisor	
Inventory losses are not investigated	
The wages control account is not reconciled each month	

(b)   Elaine Anderson, the Sales Director, has been on several management training courses and is keen to understand whether the internal controls over the shops in her area are suitable for the size of ABL, a large organisation.

Identify whether the following internal controls are more suitable for a small, medium or large organisation.

Internal control	Small	Medium	Large
Exception reporting used to investigate tills where discrepancies between cash takings and till information are higher then £5 per till per shift			
Shop managers organise compliance of food hygiene certification for staff employed in the shop			
When a shop is visited, the Regional Sales Manager reviews the value of wastage for the last month			
Certain products are reduced in price, via the till software, at a certain time of day			

Task 4

This task is about the monitoring of accounting systems and how they work in practice.

You have been asked to review the controls in the credit sales system at FBL and have established the following.

Background

- FBL's sales team deal with shop products and promotions as opposed to credit sales.

- Credit sales started when FBL's Product Development Manager was contacted by a supermarket wanting to know if they would be interested in supplying them with their fresh soups. The Product Development Manager was delighted by the opportunities in this new market and has been contacting other supermarkets and negotiating sales with them ever since.

- There are currently thirty credit customers, all of whom have deliveries on a daily basis to their regional distribution centres.

Ordering and delivery

- Purchase orders from the supermarkets are emailed to the Product Development Manager who uses the accounting system's sales order processing module to record them and communicate the orders to the Production Manager.

- Once production is complete, despatch notes are produced from the accounting software and a hard copy is given to the delivery driver who will get the customer's signature for receipt of the goods.

- The signed copies are returned to Chris Robins, the Accounts Receivable Clerk, who then uses the accounting software to raise sales invoices.

Recording receipts and account management

- The supermarkets pay by BACS on 90 day terms. The accounting software used by FBL has a receivables ledger module which is integrated with the general ledger and with the sales order processing module. Invoices raised automatically update customers' accounts.

- Mo Taylor, the General Accounts Clerk, downloads a bank statement on a daily basis and updates ledgers for receipts. Should there be disputes with customers about the quality or quantity of deliveries, these are investigated by Suri Salam, the Accounts Payable Supervisor, who will produce credit notes as required.

- Credit notes need authorisation by Will Dodds, the Management Accountant, and once authorisation has been obtained, they are posted to the customers' accounts.

- Statements are posted to customers on a monthly basis by Chris Robins, the Accounts Receivable Clerk. An aged receivables report is included in the monthly management accounts.

(a)   **(i)**   Using the table below, identify three weaknesses in FBL's credit sales system outlined above.

Weakness
1
2
3

(ii)   Evaluate the impact that each of the weaknesses could have on the organisation

Impact on the organisation
1
2
3

You have recently discovered that Anna Kolowski (Payroll Manager) has been paying a factory employee, C Arnold, £400 per week, who does not appear to work in the factory. The employee's bank details are those of Anna's aunt, Sara. She has also been overpaying another factory employee, Mary Lindberg, who Anna has worked with for many years, by £100 per month for several months.

(b) Identify which of the following procedures would detect the frauds identified above.

Procedure	Would detect	Would not detect
The Production Manager authorises all new starters and their details are input into the payroll system standing data file by the Human Resources Manager		
The wages control account is reconciled monthly		
The Assistant Accountant reviews an exception report from the payroll package each week, showing changes made from the factory clocking in system hours to actual hours paid		
Monthly production labour variances of more than 1.0% are routinely investigated		
Periodically, the Assistant Accountant spot checks the names on the gross pay report back to supporting documentation with Human Resources		
Introducing a new policy requiring accounting employees, including the Payroll Manager, to take two weeks holiday together at least once a year. Staff will be retrained to facilitate this		

Task 5

This task is about the analysis of internal controls with recommendations to improve whilst considering the impact on users.

Staff costs make up over 40% of FBL's costs and the biggest component of these costs relates to hourly paid shop workers – ie, all shop staff other than the shop managers who are salaried.

You have been asked to carry out a review of FBL's wages procedures for hourly paid shop staff and to make recommendations for improvement. The current systems are detailed below.

Recruitment and shift planning

Shop managers are responsible for the level of staffing in their shops. If they feel they need more staff, positions will be advertised and shop managers are responsible for interviewing and selecting new employees, for passing relevant documentation to HR and for arranging for new employees to attend induction training at head office. HR record details of new starters on the payroll system. HR are also responsible for removing all leavers from this system once these have been notified by shop managers.

Shop managers all use a standard spreadsheet to plan shifts. Rotas are displayed in shops two weeks in advance and the shift rota is emailed to the Payroll Clerk at the same time. Regional sales managers visit shops on pre-determined days to see how the shops are running.

When staff book holidays with their shop manager, this is recorded on an HR spreadsheet, updates of which are sent to HR on a weekly basis. HR monitor staff holidays and any sick leave, etc.

Time recording

Employees use smart cards to clock in and out of shops. Clocking data is downloaded from the clocking terminal onto a USB stick by the shop managers at the end of each day and emailed to the Payroll Clerk for analysis and processing. The Payroll Clerk uploads the data and runs exception reports to check that the data is within expected parameters. High or low numbers of hours are checked back to the shift rotas to check their validity.

Payroll – shop workers

FBL uses a standard accounting software package for payroll which is Real Time Information (RTI) compliant. This comes with automatic updates and support provided via telephone helpdesk. The Payroll Clerk exports the details of shop staff hours worked into the payroll package each day, and four working days before the end of the month, runs a monthly payroll. Check prints are produced showing employee costs for each shop as well as details for all starters and leavers.

After the payroll has been run, the Payroll Clerk produces a BACS transfer authority which is signed by two of the authorising signatories – the Financial Accountant and the Directors. Staff are paid by BACS on the last working day of the month.

(a)   (i)   Identify one strength in the procedures. Explain how this strength benefits the organisation.

      (ii)   Identify one weakness in these procedures. Describe the potential damage this weakness could cause the organisation and suggest a potential remedy.

      (iii) Identify one opportunity to improve the procedures. Explain how the procedure should be changed and how this would benefit the organisation.

      (iv) Identify one threat to the effectiveness of these procedures. Explain how the threat could damage the business and suggest an action that would reduce the risk.

A cost-benefit analysis has also been produced to support other decisions being made in FBL. Alison Davis, the Finance Director, has heard the issues identified can be categorised into Social, Corporate and Environmental. You have been asked to categorise these findings.

The following statements are the results of the cost-benefit analysis.

(b)   Identify the appropriate category for each of the following statements.

Statement	Social	Corporate	Environmental
Work experience programme for residents of local hostels, to enable them to plan a return to work			
Development of vegan ranges of soups and foods			
Locally source food ingredients			
Marketing strategy to emphasise nutritional value of products to grow sales			
Develop ranges of allergen-free foods			

Alison Davis, the Finance Director, is not familiar with PESTLE and has asked you to show which category is appropriate for the statements below.

(c)   Select categories from: Political, Economic, Social, Technological, Legal and Environmental

Statement	Category
Government policy is encouraging people to adopt healthier eating habits	
Shops will be fined if wasted food is above a certain percentage of sales	
Introducing cloud accounting, resulting in redundancies of accounting staff	
Initiative to ensure all ingredients are sustainably produced with three years	
Developing an affordable lunch range for customers with lower disposable incomes	

Answers to practice assessment 1

Task 1

(a)

Policy	Would improve	Would not improve
Implement a price increase of 5% for all existing private customers, when costs have increased by 3%		✔
Introduce speed limiters on vehicles to improve petrol consumption	✔	
Ask all qualified engineers to identify additional training requirements each year	✔	

(b)

General public	
Bank, which is tendering for ABL's business	
Shareholders	✔
Potential employee	

(c)

Performance indicator	Component required
Inventory holding period (days)	Cost of sales
Gearing	Equity
Trade receivables collection period (days)	Revenue

(d) **Internal** information does not need to comply with accounting standards. If the business is planning to open more branches, the **directors** will make this type of decision. To monitor this decision, it will use **budgeted reports by branch.**

(e)

Statement	True	False
Cloud accounting will always ensure data is more secure		✔
Cloud accounting will allow staff from branches and home to access accounting data	✔	
There are no hardware costs when cloud accounting is used		✔
The use of cloud accounting will ensure malware attacks cannot occur		✔

(f)

Statement	Risk
The password for the payroll software is written on a pad by the computer, as Priti, the Payroll Clerk, keeps forgetting it	Unauthorised physical access
Priti is emailing the payslips to staff and this week sends A Hamilton's payslip to A Hamil	Data issued in error
Tonya, the General Ledger Clerk and Cashier, is asked to open a link on an email from the bank's new email address, stating there was a problem with the weekly payroll	Denial of service
The heating engineers have been issued with tablets, to raise 'on the spot' invoices from private customers. They sometimes leave the tablet in the van overnight	Physical loss of equipment
Sanjay, the Accounts Receivable Clerk, receives an email from a new customer, asking for the bank details in readiness for payment	Phishing

(g)

Statement	Would improve	Would not improve
Presenting accounting information to branch managers using graphs	✔	
Including all the technical terms on any reports produced		✔
Creating a branch level dashboard showing sales, costs and profit on charts	✔	

(h)

Statement	True/False
A cloud accounting system that uses machine learning to post all entries will be too expensive to buy	True
The accounts clerk will not need to code each transaction, using a system with machine learning	False
Forecasting will be 100% accurate using data analytics and machine learning	False

Task 2

(a)

Weakness	Cause
When supplier statement reconciliations are performed, the reconciling items are not followed and investigated	Poor implementation of controls
The non-current assets are rarely inspected and reconciled to the non-current asset register and the general ledger	Lack of monitoring
The Operation Director is based in Exeter and rarely visits other branches, preferring to hold online meetings with other branch managers	Lack of leadership
Engineers can raise invoices, apply discounts to invoices and also take cash payments from customers	Lack of controls

(b)   *Misappropriation of assets – physical*

- Theft of inventory at housing association site, because of goods being left unattended, in an unlocked area, on the housing site.

- Goods ordered for own use due to no authorised purchase order and no robust goods received controls, comparing goods received to the purchase order at point of receipt.

- Theft of goods by customer, who could state goods have not been received or have been short delivered, due to parts being delivered directly to the customer.

Misstatement of financial statements – false accounting

- Incorrect recording of trade payables, as there is no formal control over recording supplier invoices, particularly if they are not received initially and do not send a supplier statement.

- Incorrect recording of goods received not invoiced, resulting in incorrect inventory or purchases, as no goods received system is in place.

(c)

Potential risk	Potential implications to organisation	Safeguard to minimise risk
Collusion with the customer	Loss of profit due to low pricing or high discounts given by Sales Manager	Quotations to be authorised by the Sales Director
Reputational damage	Systems supplied may be of poor quality. It may be difficult to retain the repair business if the systems are poorly made and break	Review quality of heating systems and use only those of suitable quality
Offering a five year service, parts and labour package at fixed cost on EnvironWarm, a poor quality product	The poor quality system is likely to break down, so the price paid by the customer may not cover the costs incurred	Suggest alternative system of better quality Do not offer five-year service, parts & labour packages on poor quality products

(d)

Example	Financial	Non-financial
Theft of boiler parts by branch staff	✔	
Incorrectly recording apprentice engineers' wages as selling and distribution costs in the financial statements to make the gross profit margin look higher		✔

Task 3

(a)

Weakness	Control
The wages control account has been reconciled but the reconciling items not resolved	Supervision
The Accounts Receivable Clerk can raise credit notes of any value	Authorisation and approval
Theft of spare parts from the branch stores	Physical access controls
Engineers can purchase sundry parts, if needed, from local wholesalers in their area	Organisational controls
The General Ledger Clerk and Cashier opens the post and can enter cash receipts and journals onto the cash book	Segregation of duties
The wages control account is not reconciled regularly	Check arithmetical accuracy

(b)

Internal control	Small	Large
Segregation of duties for employing new engineers, entering new employees onto the payroll system, recording hours worked by engineers and making payments to engineers		✔
Engineers can place orders for any parts required for any value	✔	
The Managing Director signs all cheques and payments	✔	
Production of monthly variance analysis reports by branch		✔

Task 4

Any three from:

(a) (i) Weakness	(a) (ii) Impact on the organisation
Engineers' timesheets filed at branch – no one at head office can determine if authorised or if amounts input agree to amounts authorised	Fraud – collusion between engineers and branch clerk could occur, so engineers are paid for hours not worked
Payroll Clerk has full user rights	The Payroll Clerk can change rates of pay, rates of pension contributions and add employees. Payroll could be incorrectly recorded or calculated. There is a fraud risk
Branch managers can add temporary staff	Fraud risk – fictitious employees, risk of breaching employment regulations if branch manager does not carry out relevant checks
Financial Accountant has only partial training on payroll software	The Financial Accountant may not be trained enough to complete the payroll and pay staff. Staff could have financial problems if they are paid late
Financial Accountant checks are limited – no check of starters and leavers, no check of deductions, or pension contributions	Payroll Clerk errors or fraud could go undetected
No overall reconciliation from Userve to payroll system for branch engineers' wages	Payroll hours could be input incorrectly onto payroll system and engineers' wages overpaid
The Financial Accountant authorises the BACS payment alone	Potential fraud by Financial Accountant – the payment could be amended and staff deliberately overpaid

(b)

Procedure	Would detect	Would not detect
Supplier payments are prepared by Hettie and checked against the bank payments by the Financial Accountant	✔	
Supplier payments are checked for numerical accuracy		✔
Only the Financial Accountant can set up new suppliers on the BACS payment *		✔
Supplier remittances are emailed to the relevant supplier		✔
The payables ledger is reviewed by the Financial Accountant periodically and any unmatched cash payments are investigated	✔	
The payables ledger control account is reconciled to the payables ledger each month		✔

* Note: This control would prevent, rather than detect, fraud.

Task 5

(a)   **(i)**   *Strength*

Engineers cannot use fuel cards to refuel own vehicles or buy additional items; breakdown of individual van mileage will highlight engineers using vans for own travel.

Benefit to organisation

Fuel purchasing system is robust making fraud difficult and costs easy to monitor.

(ii)   One from:

Purchase order module

Weakness

The lack of a purchase order system on Userve means that control over orders raised is weak.

Potential damage and remedy

When an invoice is received at head office, it is not possible to know that the goods were received on time or that they were of a suitable quality. All that can be checked is the price quoted on Userve. This could lead to ABL paying for parts which were faulty.

ABL should use a purchasing system that matches purchase orders and deliveries to purchase invoices. Deliveries of poor quality or missing items can be noted, so these are not paid for. If the firm wants to continue to use Userve, the firm may be able to commission a bespoke purchase order module which could be added to the current system.

Or

Monitoring of costs accrued at any point in time will be difficult as there will not be any visibility of goods received and not invoiced. This will reduce the accuracy of figures in management accounts and reports. It will also make the monitoring of inventory held at branches more complex.

ABL should use a purchasing system that matches purchase orders and deliveries to purchase invoices. This should have a goods received not invoiced report.

Capital expenditure approval

Weakness

ABL's systems only require the approval of one director for such orders.

Potential damage and remedy

Capital expenditure purchases frequently cost tens of thousands of pounds and significantly affect the operating efficiency and liquidity of a firm. This could lead to problems if a director fails to take into account impacts of decisions on the firm as a whole.

ABL should introduce the requirement for approval by a second director of any large capital expenditure purchases, for instance, those over £5,000 in value.

(iii) *Opportunity*

ABL could make use of its size by negotiating prices for heating and plumbing supplies centrally.

Change to procedure and benefit to organisation

At the moment branches negotiate prices individually and this will not be as effective because an individual branch has only a fraction of the buying power of the company. It may be possible to select a small number of preferred suppliers and gain improvements in both price and quality. However, due to the large area covered by branches and the rural nature of the region, the company may need to continue using several different suppliers.

(iv) *Threat*

Lack of specialist knowledge of individuals and engineers with regard to developments in microgeneration technologies could lead to the installation of systems which are dated and less efficient.

Damage to organisation and action to take to reduce the risk

Costs are continually being driven down in this sector and it is also likely that engineers will not be able to keep up-to-date with the cost effectiveness of different systems. This may result in the firm losing customers and its current good reputation for work in this sector.

The purchasing of microgeneration systems should be managed by a specialist based at head office who can advise individual engineers as required.

(b)

Statement	Social	Corporate	Environmental
Ability to recycle old plumbing for customers, when it is replaced			✔
Promotion of renewable heating systems to customers, including loyalty discounts		✔	
Training apprentices in the fitting of renewable heating systems	✔		
Investing in an appointment system, so it can communicate with customers more efficiently		✔	
Reviewing the boilers being purchased to ensure they are built in an ethical and sustainable manner by suppliers			✔

(c)

Statement	Category
More single occupancy housing leading to smaller systems being sold	Social
The falling pound resulting in higher costs of imported boiler parts, leading to higher servicing prices	Economic
Uncertainties in preferred heating systems due to changing climate change legislation	Political
Investing in a diagnostic tool that will communicate a boiler fault directly to the company	Technological
Changes to government legislation that requires new fitted boilers to meet certain efficiency criteria	Legal

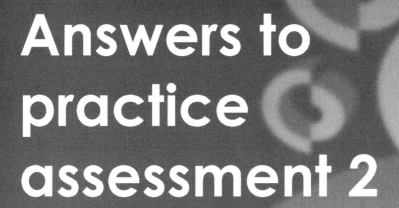

Answers to practice assessment 2

Task 1

(a)

Statement	True/ False
Decision making will be faster, as the length of scalar chain is shorter	False
The span of control is likely to be narrow	True
Productivity will be higher	True
It is more expensive to operate	True

(b) Financial information produced for **all** stakeholders must **always** be produced using ethical principles.

External stakeholders will expect financial statements to **comply** with the conceptual framework and accounting standards. This will allow stakeholders, such as the bank, to make informed decisions on **loans applications** that will enable the business to grow.

(c)

Statement	Type of financial information	Correct/Incorrect
The statement of cash flows is useful to the bank, to monitor whether CDM can repay its loans	Financial	Correct
The budgetary control reports are used to determine the overall profitability of the organisation	Management	Incorrect

(d)

Statement	True/False
Machine learning and data analytics cannot be use in the same parts of the accounting system	False
Data analytics can be useful audit tools	True
Using a system including machine learning and data analytics will de-skill the accounting staff	False
Data analytics could be used to predict future grain costs	True
Machine learning will result in less inaccurate information due to coding errors	True
Machine learning and data analytics can be used on multiple sites	True

(e)

Statement	True/False
Data dashboards will always make information more understandable to non-financial managers	False
Graphs are a key visualisation tool on a data dashboard	True
Dashboards can include performance indicators	True
Data dashboards are designed to meet non-financial users' needs	False

(f)

Statement	Required	Not required
Virus protection must be enabled and users cannot disable it	✔	
Data stored on a laptop is suitably encrypted	✔	
The laptop must be stored in a locked cupboard overnight		✔
Passwords must be changed regularly and not shared	✔	
The screen lock must be enabled at all times while the computer is unattended		✔

Task 2

(a)   The above may result in the occurrence of **monetary** fraud, that could occur as a result of **poor implementation of controls.**

In order to address this risk, you may need to implement **authorisation and approval** as soon as possible. This will ensure the impact on **liabilities** is minimised.

(b)

Weakness that may result in fraud	Internal control to prevent fraud and reason
No preferred suppliers for purchasing of non-current assets may result in Factory Manager ordering non-current assets at inflated prices in exchange for money from the supplier	Purchase orders of non-current assets to be authorised by a director to ensure non-current assets are purchased at appropriate prices
No reconciliation of physical non-current assets to non-current asset register may result in theft of non-current assets occurring and not being discovered	Periodic reconciliation and spot checks of physical non-current assets to non-current asset register and general ledger will ensure employees are deterred from stealing them
The Factory Manager can dispose of non-current assets for any value. This may result in sale of non-current assets for less than market value to related parties	Only a director can authorise disposal of a non-current asset to ensure the non-current asset is sold at market value
The Factory Manager can both order and receive non-currents assets which could result in ordering non-current assets for own use	Segregate ordering and receipt of non-current assets to ensure that items cannot be ordered for personal use and removed from the business

(c)

Situation	Rating
CDM uses weighbridges to weigh vehicles on arrival with a full load and then vehicles are weighed again on departure to calculate the weight of grain delivered. Copies of weighbridge results are passed to farmers. Purchase invoices are completed using price lists and weighbridge documentation by CDM and sent to the farmer for approval of price and weight.	High
Jayne Dudek, the Management Accountant, produces the monthly management accounts. She enters journals to the general ledger, along with Oliver Matthews, the Finance Director.	Medium
Each day the post is opened by two people, who record all cash receipts on a receipts list. These are entered into the cash book by Susanne Dobson, the Assistant Accountant, which automatically updates the receivables ledger. The posted cash receipts are agreed to the receipts list by Oti Adeyemi, the Financial Accountant daily.	Low

(d)   Any one from:

Risk – customers place orders they cannot pay for

Monitor

- Customers who exceed their credit limit
- How much we expected to sell and receive vs how much we did sell and receive

Review

- Receivables ledger to determine how many customers have exceeded the credit limit
- Internal audit walk through test to identify area that needs additional controls
- The level of irrecoverable debts

Report

- Use software to highlight customers who exceed credit limit
- Produce monthly chart to show irrecoverable debts
- Monthly report of customers over credit limit and the exceeded amounts

Risk – Credit notes issued fraudulently

Monitor

- Level of credit notes under £500 raised each month
- How much we expected to issue in credit notes and how much we did

Review

- The number and amount of credit notes issued
- Internal audit walk through test to identify area that needs additional controls
- The reason for credit notes issued

Report

- Use software to highlight credit notes issued and divide them between above and below £500
- Produce table/chart to show credit notes issued
- Monthly report of credit notes issued

Risk – Excessive discounts given, either in error or fraudulently

Monitor

- Level of discounts offered each month
- How much we expected discounts to be and how much they were

Review

- The discounts applied to sales invoices
- Internal audit walk through test to identify area that needs additional controls
- The sales per month for customers compared with previous months

Report

- Use software to determine discounts given
- Produce table/chart to show discounts given
- Monthly report of discounts given

Task 3

(a)

Internal Control	Purpose	Suitable – Yes/No
Regularly reconcile the VAT control account	Prevent and detect fraud and error	Yes
The directors are the only authorised signatories on the bank accounts	Compliance	No*
Monthly management accounts are produced and reviewed	Safeguard assets	No**
The new accounting system is cloud based and is backed up automatically	Facilitate operations	Yes

*suitable to safeguard assets; **suitable for ensuring quality of internal reporting

(b)

Internal control	Cash-based	Credit-based	Online
Customers are subject to rigorous credit checks with a credit agency prior to orders being placed		✔	
Payment is made prior to the order being confirmed and delivery details being obtained			✔
Customers pay for the goods at point of order and collection	✔		

(c)

Improvement	Would promote	Would not promote
Employees with hybrid or electric cars are given priority parking	✔	
All non-grain suppliers are chosen solely based on lowest price		✔
All new starters complete an induction programme	✔	

Task 4

(a)   Deficiencies

- No robust check of credit limit before accepting an order

- Errors are possible in completing the worksheet, leading to under or over-ordering

- Human error could lead to some sales orders being missed and not emailed to production, or to some emails to production being delayed

- No despatch notes produced for customers to sign – customers could deny having received the goods

- Details of some despatches might not be emailed to the Accounts Receivable Clerk, or there may be some delay in emailing details of the despatches

- The Accounts Receivable Clerk is responsible for creating all invoices and credit notes

Causes

- Lack of formal procedures over enforcing credit limits

- Lack of sales ordering – no sales order numbers

- Lack of formal procedures over communicating sales orders to production

- Lack of formal system for recording deliveries/despatch of good

- Lack of segregation of duties

Impact

- Sales made to a bad credit risk, and subsequent irrecoverable debt

- Errors in pricing or amounts of VAT could cause conflict with customers. If a lower price is quoted than due, the company will probably have to honour this price even if the sale then becomes loss making

- Customers will be dissatisfied if goods are not received or received late and they could change to other suppliers

- Production will find it harder to schedule output effectively if orders are not notified promptly

- CDM will not be able to bring successful legal action against the customer in the event of the customer refusing to pay

- Sales might not be invoiced, causing loss to the company. Sales might be invoiced late – this will affect cash flow as payments will be made based on invoice date

- If the Accounts Receivable Clerk were acting in collusion with a customer, invoices could simply not be raised. Alternatively, the Accounts Receivable Clerk could issue credit notes to cancel amounts outstanding in return for back-handers from customers

(b)

Statement	True/False
The most expensive accounting system will always be the best	False
Electronic invoicing is more cost effective than paper-based invoicing	True
Qualified accounting staff should help CDM support ethical principles	True

(c) The accounting system must be **reviewed regularly** to ensure it **meets the needs of the organisation.**

Task 5

(a) **(i)**

Costs	£
Training costs (£1,600 x 4 staff) + (£800 x 2 staff)	8,000
Load contracts onto new system	6,000
Software licence	15,000
Hardware upgrades	17,500
Benefits	
Cost saving of grain purchases (£12,400,000 x 0.5%)	62,000
Overtime saving	3,000
(Net cost)/benefit	18,500 benefit

(ii)

Any six from:

- Will the buyers be unhappy to lose the overtime which they have been paid for several years?
- Will the buyers and directors be able to use the new system effectively?
- Will the forecasting be more accurate and the savings in grain purchases be realised?
- Will the IT training be sufficient to meet the needs of the staff?
- How will the transition to the new forecasting system be managed?
- What controls will be in place to load in the existing contracts?
- Reporting information is more extensive, so should enable better decision-making.

(iii)

Any two from:

- CDM should invest in the GrainStore system, as should result in a net benefit of £18,500.

- It should reduce grain purchase costs.

- It should improve decision-making on purchases, due to better reporting information.

(b)

Concern	Yes/No
Data could be lost or transferred incorrectly	Yes
The old system may be used for longer than expected	No
Controls may not operate effectively	Yes
Ethical principles may be breached	No
The service to customers or suppliers may be adversely affected	Yes
Staff may become demotivated	Yes

(c)

Characteristic	Associated / Not associated
Staff may be overwhelmed with changes	Not associated
Staff will determine when the next phase is implemented	Associated
Data will be transferred between the old and new systems	Associated
Will reduce staff productivity temporarily	Associated
Risk of data corruption is increased	Not associated
Higher costs due to inputting information twice	Not associated

Answers to practice assessment 3

Task 1

(a)

	Would improve	Would not improve
Give unsold food to local hostels and food banks	✔	
Set a target to employ at least one apprentice at every location within the next two years	✔	
Implement productivity bonuses on evening production shifts only		✔

(b)

Customers	
Bank	
Employee	✔
Suppliers	

(c)

Performance indicator	Component required
Quick (acid test) ratio	Inventories
Return on capital employed	Operating profit
Current ratio	Current liabilities
Trade payables collection period (days)	Cost of sales

(d)

Purpose	Type of data analytic
Produce budgetary reports of budget to actual information	Descriptive
Recommend new types of products to make and sell, based on internal and external research	Prescriptive
Find the reason for adverse production variances	Diagnostic
Forecast sales by product type	Predictive

(e) Budgetary control information may be more easily understood by shop and production managers if it is presented **using a data dashboard.** Non-financial managers may require information presented **in a clear, uncluttered format.**

To ensure the information is understandable, you should **discuss it with managers with limited financial knowledge.**

(f)

Statement	True/False
Cloud accounting is not compatible with data analytics	False
Cloud accounting will result in higher hardware costs	False
Staff productivity is unlikely to be affected, if remote access is stable and reliable	True
Data is backed up automatically, resulting in less likelihood of data loss	True
Cloud accounting includes machine learning, which reduces errors	True

(g)

Statement	Risk
Anya Kolowski, the Payroll Manager, emailed A Jones's payslip to B Jones	Data issued in error
The Production Manager has shared his password with the Factory Supervisor, to enable production to operate efficiently	Unauthorised physical access
Mo Taylor, the General Accounts Clerk, receives an email from the bank, asking him to click on a link to confirm the bank details for a BACS payment	Phishing
Shop managers use laptops during the day. The laptop is left unattended on the desk at the back of the shop office	Physical loss of equipment

Task 2

(a)

Weakness	Cause
Management and supervision of shops is often remote	Lack of leadership
There is no limit on the amount the Production Manager can order from suppliers of raw materials	Lack of controls
The Production Director infrequently investigates the materials usage and labour utilisation variances in the factory	Lack of monitoring
When the VAT return is completed and reconciled to the VAT control account, reconciling items are not followed and cleared	Poor implementation of controls

(b)   Any two from:

Misappropriation of assets – monetary

- The Production Manager could place orders of ingredients for the factory at a high price, paid by FBL, in exchange for money from the supplier.

- The Production Manager could approve purchase invoices where goods have not been received, or the price is incorrect, in exchange for money from the supplier.

Misappropriation of assets – inventory

- Items could be purchased for own use by the shop managers, as there is no segregation between ordering and receipt of shop items.

- Theft of shop items due to shop inventory being stored in an unlocked area at the back of the shop.

Misstatement of financial statements – false accounting

- Incorrect recording of shop inventory due to no physical inventory count, item by item, by location, so profits or losses could be under or overstated.

- Incorrect recording of goods received not invoiced, resulting in incorrect inventory or purchases, as no goods received system is in place for either the factory or the shops.

- Incorrect recording of trade payables as no segregation between ordering and authorising invoices for purchases by the factory or the shops.

(c)

Potential risk	Potential implications to organisation	Safeguard to minimise risk
Production of inventory by the factory, as recommended by the till information, when it is not required	Loss of profit due to production of goods not required, which may then be wasted, resulting in lower profits	Staff to be trained on the till system, so information produced by it will be accurate
Unable to take credit card payments for sales	Lost sales that day, resulting in lower profits. Loss of future sales – customer will go elsewhere	Ensure shop can use both internet and a mobile phone link to take payments
Reputational damage OR legal fines	Staff are not being paid according to their contract and may be paid below minimum wage, resulting in fines	Regional managers to spot check where breaks are worked and compare it back to payroll. Disciplinary action for shop managers who deduct break hours

(d)

Example	Financial	Non-financial
Stealing cash takings from the till in the shop	✔	
Adjusting the depreciation rates on non-current assets so the depreciation charge is lower in the year, overstating profits, to earn a company-wide staff bonus	✔	

Task 3

(a)

Weakness	Control
Bank reconciliations are produced by Mo Taylor, the General Accounts Clerk, who is unqualified	Personnel
The Accounts Payables Supervisor, Suri Salam, posts purchase invoices and payments to the payables ledger	Segregation of duties
The payroll computer is kept in an unlocked office	Physical access controls
Casual production staff are employed by the Factory Supervisor	Authorisation and approval
Inventory losses are not investigated	Management
The wages control account is not reconciled each month	Check arithmetical accuracy

(b)

Internal control	Small	Medium	Large
Exception reporting used to investigate tills where discrepancies between cash takings and till information are higher then £5 per till per shift			✔
Shop managers organise compliance of food hygiene certification for staff employed in the shop	✔*		
When a shop is visited, the Regional Sales Manager reviews the value of wastage for the last month		✔**	
Certain products are reduced in price, via the till software, at a certain time of day			✔

*Medium and large organisations are likely to control this risk centrally.

**This would not be needed in a small organisation. A large organisation would monitor this by shop on a daily basis.

Task 4

(a) Three of the following:

(i) Weakness	(ii) Impact on organisation
Product Development Manager negotiates all terms	Risk of fraud – Product Development manager could offer favourable prices and rates to customers in return for money
Customers are not credit checked in any way before accounts are opened	Sales made to a bad credit risk and subsequent irrecoverable receivables
No authorised credit limits	No limit on potential irrecoverable receivables risk
No formal credit agreements are produced for signature by the customer before trading commences	No formal contract set up defining terms of trade Possible problems should disputes arise and need to be resolved in court
Staff do not confirm the status of the customer's account before accepting an order	Sales could be made to a bad credit risk, and result in an irrecoverable receivable
No member of staff is specifically responsible for monitoring customer accounts and chasing receivables	Overdue invoices will remain undetected for a long time Customers who delay payment will not be held to account This may encourage late payments by customers who could afford to pay but want to maximise their own cash flow Receivables may become irrecoverable, harming profits and cash flow
No procedures for chasing accounts or for putting customers' accounts on stop	Sales may be made to customers who cannot pay for them Potential irrecoverable receivables Profits and receivables will be overstated until irrecoverable receivable is written off
No limit on credit notes issued	The Management Accountant could incorrectly issue credit notes for high values If they collude with a customer, this could result in fraud Profits may be lost unnecessarily
Sales order processing module is not integrated with the accounting system	Sales invoices raised could be for the wrong price Profits could be lost Customers may be unhappy if they are over-charged

(b)

Procedure	Would detect	Would not detect
The Production Manager authorises all new starters and their details are input into the payroll system standing data file by the Human Resources Manager		✔*
The wages control account is reconciled monthly	✔	
The Assistant Accountant reviews an exception report from the payroll package each week, showing changes made from the factory clocking in system hours to actual hours paid	✔	
Monthly production labour variances of more than 1.0% are routinely investigated		✔**
Periodically, the Assistant Accountant spot checks the names on the gross pay report back to supporting documentation with Human Resources	✔	
Introducing a new policy requiring accounting employees, including the Payroll Manager, to take two weeks holiday together at least once a year. Staff will be retrained to facilitate this	✔	

* This would prevent the fraud but not detect it.
** Due to the size of the factory workforce, it is unlikely the additional payments would create this size of variance, so the procedure would not detect it.

Task 5

(a)   (i)   One strength from:

Payroll software package

Strength

The payroll software package used is efficient and ensures compliance with RTI requirements.

Benefit to organisation

Changes to tax rates and allowances are adjusted through automatic updates so FBL can be sure that the right amounts of taxes are being charged and paid to the government.

Segregation of duties - shop payroll

Strength

There is segregation of duties between HR who set up and remove shop employees on the payroll system and the Payroll Clerk who records the hours worked.

Benefit to organisation

This reduces the risk of fraud. A fictitious shop employee could not be paid unless there was collusion between HR and the Payroll Clerk, making this type of fraud much more unlikely.

Payment of payroll by BACS

Strength

The payment of wages by BACS, rather than cash or cheque.

Benefit to organisation

This payment method is far less time consuming to administer than payments by cash or cheques and the risk of theft or fraud is a lot lower. In addition, bank charges for automated payments are lower than for cash or cheque payments.

(ii)   One weakness from:

Shop managers determine staffing levels

Weakness

Reliance on shop managers for identifying optimum staffing level for shop.

Potential damage and remedy

Staffing levels could be too low or too high, resulting in overstaffing or understaffing. This could also frustrate shop workers and antagonise customers. Regional sales managers could carry out unannounced shop visits to determine if the staffing level is correct. Managers who are under- or over-staffing could then be trained.

Payroll data transfer using USB

Weakness

Shop managers transfer clocking in data to a USB and email it to Payroll Clerk.

Potential damage and remedy

Reliance on shop managers transferring clocking data to USB and emailing to Payroll Clerk. This is time consuming and there is a risk of loss of data. Integrating the clocking in system to the payroll system would remove this issue.

Clocking in cards

Weakness

Staff could swipe friends' smartcards and make it look as if they arrived or left work earlier or later than actually occurred.

Potential damage and remedy

This would increase the wages costs of the company. Change clocking in system to one with a biometric log in – such as fingerprint.

Shop managers inform HR when staff leave

Weakness

Shop managers are responsible for notifying HR of leavers.

Potential damage and remedy

They could collude with staff who have left, not report when they leave and continue to clock them in and out to defraud the company.

Regional sales managers could make unannounced visits and check which staff are working. Similar shops could be compared to determine staffing levels and likely staff costs. Shops with high staff costs could be audited by the regional sales managers.

(iii)   One opportunity from:

Workforce management system

Opportunity

FBL could invest in a workforce management system to automate staffing levels and rotas.

Change to procedure and benefit to organisation

This would help to identify the best staffing levels for each shop and the most economic shift patterns. This would improve the control of shop workers' wages and could reduce staff costs, increasing profits.

Biometric clocking in system technology (if clocking in system is not used as a weakness)

Opportunity

FBL could upgrade clocking system to use biometric data such as facial recognition or fingerprints.

Change to procedure and benefit to organisation

Staff could clock in using the new biometric system. This would eliminate the risk of employees clocking in or out for each other and the possibility of paying for hours not worked.

(iv) *Threat*

FBL could be at risk of legal proceedings if shop managers fail to properly carry out employment checks – such as that a prospective worker has the right to work in the UK – or if they breach some other aspect of employment law such as the Equalities Act.

Damage to organisation and action to take to reduce the risk

Legal proceedings would be expensive and would damage the reputation of the business.

FBL needs to ensure that all shop managers receive adequate HR training before interviewing any prospective employees. HR must also review all paperwork to ensure it is in order for every starter.

(b)

Statement	Social	Corporate	Environmental
Work experience programme for residents of local hostels, to enable them to plan a return to work	✔		
Development of vegan ranges of soups and foods		✔	
Locally source food ingredients			✔
Marketing strategy to emphasise nutritional value of products to grow sales		✔	
Develop ranges of allergen-free foods		✔	

(c)

Statement	Category
Government policy is encouraging people to adopt healthier eating habits	Political
Shops will be fined if wasted food is above a certain percentage of sales	Legal
Introducing cloud accounting, resulting in redundancies of accounting staff	Technological
Initiative to ensure all ingredients are sustainably produced with three years	Environmental
Developing an affordable lunch range for customers with lower disposable incomes	Economic

for your notes

for your notes

for your notes

for your notes

for your notes

for your notes

for your notes

for your notes